Release the Hostage

*Break the shackles and
be the inspirational CEO*

Jagdish Kini

Release the Hostage
Copyright © 2022 Jagdish Kini
First published in 2022

Print: 978-1-76124-025-6
E-book: 978-1-76124-026-3
Hardback: 978-1-76124-024-9

All rights reserved. No part of this book may be reproduced, stored in a retrieval system, or transmitted by any means (electronic, mechanical, photocopying, recording, or otherwise) without written permission from the author.

Because of the dynamic nature of the Internet, any web addresses or links contained in this book may have changed since publication and may no longer be valid. The information in this book is based on the author's experiences and opinions. The views expressed in this book are solely those of the author and do not necessarily reflect the views of the publisher; the publisher hereby disclaims any responsibility for them.

The author of this book does not dispense any form of medical, legal, financial, or technical advice either directly or indirectly. The intent of the author is solely to provide information of a general nature to help you in your quest for personal development and growth. In the event you use any of the information in this book, the author and the publisher assume no responsibility for your actions. If any form of expert assistance is required, the services of a competent professional should be sought.

Publishing information
Publishing, design, and production facilitated by Passionpreneur Publishing,
A division of Passionpreneur Organization Pty Ltd, ABN: 48640637529

www.PassionpreneurPublishing.com
Melbourne, VIC | Australia

TABLE OF CONTENTS

What leaders think about working with Jagdish   V

Acknowledgements   IX

Introduction   1

1. Get up and finish the race   3
2. Failure is not the opposite of success, but part of the journey   17
3. Unleash your Potential   33
4. Create awareness, it is the foundation   47
5. Slow down if you want to go fast   69
6. Communications connect people   85
7. Structure trumps chaos   101
8. Trust this Glue   115
9. Vulnerability is a strength   129
10. Being Abundant   141

11	Be the secure base	155
12	Be the two-minute coach	167
13	Don't predict the future, create it	185

Authors Bio   199

WHAT LEADERS THINK ABOUT WORKING WITH JAGDISH

There are few leaders like Jagdish who are driven by ethics, passion and positive energy! I had the good fortune of observing him from the trenches as he built Airtel as the top mobile brand in South India. Anyone reading his book is sure to benefit greatly from his vast experience not only in the industry but also as a world-renowned executive coach.

—R G Srinivas, Chief Revenue Officer, Tibil Solutions

"I learnt a lot through frameworks like vulnerability, speed of presence, SCARF, individual and group saboteurs and level 3 conversations etc. It helped me gain a deeper understanding of different aspects beyond my technical aspects of my business and work. It helped me be a lot more kind to myself and others around me. Thinking about my family and long-term goals helped me take better control of my personal and professional lives. I am glad to have begun this journey of practicing mindfulness in every aspect of my life. Thank you Jagdish"

—Mukesh Sharma, Partner Menterra, Impacting India

Jagdish is a compassionate, highly intelligent and deeply experienced mind. His focussed yet friendly, open attitude adds it all to make him a great coach / teacher I have ever met.

Jagdish helped to bring out the best in me by the most subtle and sensitive techniques through well planned and organised sessions. It was almost impossible for many to even tell me about this streak of sarcasm as an anger expression substitute in difficult situations. The way Jagdish managed to convey me this was almost spiritual and helped me win over my Saboteur.

Coaching sessions with Jagdish were one of the best learnings for me – I achieved far beyond the objective and it impacted me deeper in conscientious. My questions, unrequired extended logical reasoning and even arguments with him on the topic were all met with a smile and satisfactory and convincing responses.

The end of the formal coaching session was a beginning of a great relationship with him as a guide and mentor and a friend for ever.

—Vikas Shirsat, Senior V P and Managing Director, Jubilant Biosys

"I haven't seen another leader who trusts his/her team so completely as Jagdish. The faith reposed in you not only brings out the best in you but builds a sense of personal loyalty and an ultimate winning attitude. I personally tried to emulate the philosophy of the Jagdish School of Management all through my career and cherished every moment of it!"

—K Srinivas, MD & CEO, BTI Payments Private Limited

"I had the privilege of being coached by Jagdish during my CXO stint at Diageo, India. He helped me understand my life purpose and then went on to cocreate a path to help me live my purpose. Jagdish is an enviable combination of a successful business leader and an effective coach. Young leaders can learn a lot just from his life experiences. I will forever cherish my association with him"

—Kedar Ulman, Chief Supply Officer, Diageo India

I was blessed to be Mr. Kini's mentee way back in 2015 for CXO coaching. While this engagement lasted for 6-7 months, it has left lifelong imprints on my professional and personal life.

It made me let-go a lot of what wasn't so important – gave me a lot of "me" time to reflect on situations and think of different perspectives. This experience taught the true value and significance of "coaching" and I attribute a lot to Mr. Kini (fondly call him Chief).

Wishing him good luck and god bless. His learnings and experience will be of immense value to all.

—Anurag Gupta

"I had the pleasure of being coached by Jagdish during some difficult times in my career as MD & CEO of Sterlite Power. Jagdish is extremely well read and has a knack to weave in all his spiritual and psychology learnings into his coaching. I found him always to be focused and never digressing from what truly matters. His nudge towards "speed of presence" which comes from mindfulness practise, is something that I hope to keep forever"

—Pratik Agarwal, MD & CEO Sterlite Power

It was a great learning experience working with Jagdish. He had the ability to soar and swoop in fairly short notice, helping us to stay nimble. He also kept reminding all of us about the importance of respecting the customers. He could connect with employees across all levels. However, his biggest contribution to me personally was to help me set goals that would look impossible! He would encourage and push us to take audacious goals without fear, even his follow-ups would be on the effort put in for the task rather than focus on the failure to achieve those goals. This taught me to set goals that would seem impossible and rally the team towards achieving those.

—Elango Thambiah, Co-founder, The Ganga Foundation

"I am very pleased to see that Jagdish Kini has decided to write a book on the experiences he has had in his distinguished career.

I have had the pleasure of working closely with Jagdish and was always impressed with his extraordinary leadership skills and the way he would motivate his team and align them to a common goal. He very effectively played the role of a mentor and a director in being innovative in approach and making each and every member of the team to own that initiative as his own. He was thus, not surprisingly, not only very successful but also very popular.

I hope his book teaches this rare art to young leaders."

—Akhil Gupta , Group Vice Chairman Bharti Airtel

ACKNOWLEDGEMENTS

This book is an effort to bring into perspective the learning I have from the many truly amazing people I have met and interacted in a deep way. The Insights I have had from these interactions have impacted my life deeply and have brought immense satisfaction and joy to my life.

My teachers Fr. Nereis, Usha Nair, Mr. Tiwary, at school, Dr. BSKS Chopra, P C Narayan, Arun Nanda at the Symbiosis Institute of Business Management Pune, my professors at INSEAD – Fontainebleau, Professors and Facilitators at IIM-B, IIM-A, SHL, Center for Creative Leadership- Colorado Springs USA who helped me understand Business and Life with a deep sense of gratitude is very fulfilling.

I have been blessed in my career that I had the opportunity to work with some fantastic leaders. Mickey Dayal who gave me my first lesson in Business at Siemens. Gurcharan Das who gave me the wings and the wind under my wings at Proctor and Gamble. Keki Pardiwala, Sumit Bhattacharya, Samar Mazumdar who shaped my early career at Procter and Gamble. H Mouvillier, and Jean Jacque Mason De Blaise, who helped me believe in myself as a Leader and to believe that I could create the future for L'Oréal and for myself. Brandy Gill who made it easy and enjoyable for me to slip into the role of a Managing Director at Gillette. Sunil Mittal who gave me the space to operate, who had my back and gave me the courage to disrupt myself and the structures to create the future.

RCS (Results coaching) for the rigour it taught me in Coaching, The Live workshops I attended with Marshall Goldsmith helped to demystify coaching. Leon Vanderpol for the experience in Deep Intensive Coaching. The Points of You which gave me another perspective to coaching specially when the coachee feels stuck. My Internet Gurus Simon Sinek, Judith Glaser, Shirzad Chamine, Trace Hobson, Dr. Brenie Brown, Dr. Bruce Lipton, David Clutterberg among others. My clients have been the biggest resource for my learning and reinventing myself to be a better coach. I have gained more from the relationship than they could have. My Two years as President of the ICF chapter Bangalore, the members, and the Chai pe Charcha (Discussion over Tea) have led to deep learning and honing my skills as a coach.

Thanks to my esteemed client Mahindra and Mahindra I had the opportunity to meet and learn from George Kohlrieser the world-renowned hostage negotiator and Author and other Professors from IMD and Yale. Through my association with CoachA of Japan, TLC of USA, Acuity of UK and Knolskape I have had the privilege to coach International Leaders and learnt through interactions with international coaches.

My associates and professional partners at Enterprise5C, Samita who helped in facilitating workshops with me, and a fellow coach Surekha Poddar always believed and pushed me in different ways to put pen to paper and share my thoughts.

ACKNOWLEDGEMENTS

My Book coach Harika and Mustafa who have helped to conceive this and gave me the strength to put pen to paper. The first step was the most difficult made easy by Mustafa and his team.

My Family has been my strength through my life and career. My parents instilled the values by which I live. My Wife Anjali on whose judgement I have tremendous faith, has been my biggest support and my biggest critique. She has kept me grounded and ensured that I fly up above to have a clear view of what was important for us as a family. Our daughters Anushree and Deepali have always supported every decision of ours and continue to give us tremendous joy. Our grandson Kabir who never fails to be courteous and makes me feel like a hero, whilst the truth is I am learning from him. He has taught me the true meaning of Gratitude.

Despite all the learning, insights, and support from such learned people I am sure you would find something in these pages you may not agree with or nuances of the language which may have missed my attention. Please forgive me for the mistakes and would request you to pick up what works for you and to run with it.

INTRODUCTION

Faith is taking the first step even when you don't see the whole staircase.

—Martin Luther King

Congratulations for taking an important step in achieving the goal of your life time. Just by picking up this book, you have shown that you value your dream highly and would explore possibilities and strive hard to make it come true, and that's commendable!

It is normal to move at a tangent to your career goal, but what is important is to design strategies to get back to the straight line. In order to help you with that in a seamless manner and guide you towards your lifetime goal of becoming a CEO of your own company, or an organization you've been passionately working for, I have come up with this book.

When I decided to write the book, I have heard many people ask me questions like:

Is it like a coaching manual?

Is it a self-help book?

Are there your stories, we have heard so many of them in your workshops?

So, before we move further, let me tell you one thing. *Release the Hostage* is a play book to building resilient teams that are searching for nothing less than a win-win result. The content you read here is meticulously drafted with an aim to help young leaders evolve from being a Good to a Great Leader.

I have shared several stories from my life to help the readers realise that what they are going through is part of life and can be managed to their advantage, and I hope you benefit from it.

In my decades of experience managing companies, I have learned the secrets of co-creating successful teams and propel the company and its people to success. I realized that there are countless people like me, who dream of doing the same, and that's where my purpose took life — to help these young leaders achieve what they desperately want/dream of in life, and become even more successful.

Before you start, remember, this is just a playbook to guide you through the process and bring clarity. It's up to you as to how you take these learnings forward and put into good use.

So, are you ready to achieve your life goal of becoming a successful CEO? Go ahead and turn the page.

1

GET UP AND FINISH THE RACE

It was Bombay in 1965 and I was ten. India was at war with Pakistan and there was fear and tension on the streets. At home, we covered our windows with black paper and the top halves of car headlights were painted black, to help hide them from intruders from above. The neighbourhood had drilled for air-raids and when the sirens went off everyone knew what to do.

Around 4 pm one afternoon, the sirens sounded and people scrambled from their houses to the shelters. As we ran, three fighter planes flew above us in a dogfight. People said it was two of our Gnats chasing down the Pakistani plane that had set the sirens going. It was then that my ten-year-old self knew, I wanted to become a fighter pilot.

For seven long years, I nurtured the dream of the blue uniform, the power, and the thrill of breaking the sound barrier. But it wasn't meant to be. I was seventeen and in my first year at college and my dream was shattered when I didn't make the cut for the National

Defence Academy. I felt broken, but I remembered what Mr Andrade, my school sports teacher, had told me: finish what you have started. I knew that I needed to get up, keep going, and finish the race. I had to find a new dream.

While I had been dreaming of uniforms and jet fuel, my older sister had begun studying medicine. A brilliant student, she became my new role model. My father encouraged me to follow her path, sowing the seeds of another dream. During my final year of school, the students in my year level took aptitude tests to guide our future education and career choices. According to my test results, I was suited to becoming a surgeon or a carpenter. I latched onto this endorsement and my father's encouragement to consider Medicine and, having enjoyed studying biology, I started to dream in earnest of becoming a surgeon. But this dream was shattered, too, when I didn't make the cut to enter medical studies.

I found myself at a dead end. I was eighteen, with no career in sight. With the loss of my childhood dreams, I was searching for a new goal to reach for. For young men like me, the choice of professional careers was between engineering, medicine, or accountancy. With medicine out of reach and lacking a clear direction, I switched my focus to the pure sciences and enrolled in a science degree, in physics and chemistry.

Once I had chosen a path and started university, I fell to dreaming again. Dreaming is good for the young, and I had many dreams. Having considered myself a sportsman and representing my school in several sports, I continued to dream of a sporting career during my university years and represented my college in cricket, basketball, and badminton. Cricket was closest to my heart but, while I put in the time to practise the skills of the game, my playing time was limited. My parents had inculcated in me the importance of education as the only reliable ticket to a professional career. So it was only after attending lectures and completing my studies that I practised and played, making it to the reserves of the University team.

My university years went quickly and soon I had graduated. The reality of life hit me hard when my dad asked, 'What next? Briefly, I contemplated enrolling in a master's degree so that I could continue to play cricket for the university. But I had to face the fact that there were younger students with more talent and commitment. It was only later in life that I realised the real meaning of passion and hard practise. With hindsight, I realised my love for cricket and other sports was never more than a hobby and a pleasant dream, not a passion that drove me to make it a career. It took time to realise that achieving a dream calls for complete focus and zero tolerance for distraction.

So, I was back to my father's question. I was not enthused by the thought of completing a master's degree to work as a lab assistant, or completing a doctorate to pursue an academic career. Once again, I was a mess. The feeling wasn't new, but somewhere I had begun to understand that I needed to accept the situation. If I accepted where I was, slowly but surely clarity would emerge and I would find another path forward.

Before clarity had emerged, I talked with my father. While he wasn't part of the top leadership team at Burma Shell or considered a fast-track manager, he was a happy employee, full of gratitude. He was a diligent employee who was committed to his work and the organisation he worked for. For him, work was worship. Despite my dreams and indecision, I had learned from my father the value of dedication. I told him I wanted to look for a job and start my career. It was as though I had given up on working out what I should pursue and couldn't imagine what was possible beyond what I already knew. I had resigned myself to following the same career path I knew my father had navigated so successfully. But I hadn't expected my father's response. He said, matter of factly, that he would not help me in any way to get a job.

At the time, I wasn't sure whether it was a lack of contacts or that he did not want to use his contacts to put me forward. But what he did was tremendous. Only later, I realised that my father intended to give me independence, and this was central to his value system and beliefs about the importance of work. By making me find my way, he helped me build confidence in my strength and ability to get a job and forge a career.

Every morning my father gave me ten rupees and said, 'Son, all the best! Go get yourself a job.' The return bus fare from my parents' house to Bombay's business district was five rupees. A lunch plate in an Udupi restaurant cost 4.50 rupees. Every morning, I took the bus to the business district with my resumes in hand and knocked on company doors. If I liked what I saw from outside, I handed the receptionist a copy of my resume and ask about jobs they could offer to a fresh graduate. In the middle of the day, I bought my lunch plate and, at the end of the day, I took the bus back home.

I started dreaming again and dreaming big. My new dream was to work for a large and successful organisation, and if they were a world leader that would be the icing on the cake. As it turned out, I would work with the world's No 1 companies throughout my career. But I'm getting ahead of myself.

In no time, a month had passed with me getting dressed and ready every morning for an interview that might or might not be offered, and getting on the bus to the business district with money for lunch from my father. But still no success. I had given my resume to more than thirty companies. One job that looked promising was as a medical representative for Glaxo. I shared this news with my older sister who was on the verge of graduating with her medical degree. 'So you would visit doctors and then detail the product benefits?' I was confused at what sounded like her disapproval. I needed a job, but when the offer came, I couldn't get my sister's question out of my head. I declined the offer, not at all confident that I had done the right thing.

Around the same time, I received a call inviting me to complete the written test for graduate trainees at Siemens. I completed the test and follow-up interviews and was thrilled to be offered a traineeship. I had landed my first job and I had earned it through persistence. My career had begun. I was posted to the Siemens factory at Kalwe outside of Thane and earned a salary of six hundred rupees a month. I felt like I had conquered the world.

At Siemens, I made some dear friends for life. Ravi Thatte and Mukund Marathe ignited the fire in me to continue studying as I worked my way up. I followed their example and started a postgraduate course in cost and works accounting. However, I soon realised that Ravi and Mukund were far more committed to study than I ever was. It just wasn't my strength and, without a background in commerce, the course was not easy. I made another close friend in Srinivas, a chartered accountant who had joined the company on the same day as me. Srinivas advised me about the Indian Institutes of Management, known as IIMs, which were prestigious institutes and would help move my career forward. Once again, I began to dream.

I sat for the entrance exams for the IIMs and managed to clear them, but it was a different story when it came to the group discussion element of the admissions process. I had limited experience in this kind of activity and it suddenly seemed as though the world was conspiring against my every effort to get ahead. For the next three years, I tried and failed to get into the IIMs. Every year, the group discussions were dominated by graduates from St Stephens of Delhi or the IITs. No one else could get a word in, and applicants like me were reduced to being spectators with front-row seats.

On my third round of attempts, I decided to try other institutes as well as the IIMs. I applied to Jamnalal Bajaj (JBIMS) and the Symbiosis Institute of Business Management (SIBM). At Jamnalal Bajaj, I did well in both the written test and group discussion. After the group discussion, the evaluator told me that I had done well and should be happy with my performance. With this encouragement, I looked forward to a positive outcome, but my name did not appear on the list of successful applicants. However, I was accepted at SIBM and was optimistic that this would be my next step forward. I decided to leave Siemens and go back to university for two years.

When I shared my plans with my father, he reminded me that I was doing well at Siemens and if I continued to work with commitment, I could advance and do well. He was concerned that SIBM was still a young institution and I would be in only the third cohort of students to graduate. My father reminded me that their placement record was not impressive and asked me a question that made me think: 'Do you think you will land a job that pays you more than what you are getting today?'

After I completed my MBA with SIBM, including successful campus placements, I joined RHL (P&G) as a management trainee. My stipend was 1620 rupees per month, 20 rupees more than my last drawn salary with Siemens. My dad smiled.

From dreams to reality

Growing up, my wish list was long. But the first twenty-four years of my life went by without any of my dreams giving me joy. Like most people, I blamed everybody but myself. If I didn't do well in sport, I blamed the equipment. If I didn't do well at school, it was the teacher's fault, and so on. Even at the IIM group discussions when the students from Stephen's ganged up against the IITians, I protested at the unfairness. I used to believe that there was only one code and that if everybody followed it, I would succeed. The world had to be fair, or so I thought.

It was at SIBM that I developed some of the deepest relationships of my life. One of them was with Anjali, my wife of thirty-seven years. Falling in love transforms you. I was learning and going through a deep transformation. If I have been able to stay as rocksteady on this journey as I appeared to others, it is thanks to my soulmate Anjali. When I shared my anger and frustrations, she listened. When I shared my fears, she comforted me. But she also confronted me about my failures and helped me face each challenge.

While I changed at SIBM, it wasn't consistent. To become a reality, dreams need effort and perseverance. At SIBM I learned that perhaps it wasn't everyone else's fault and that I had not been focused enough or done enough to realise my past dreams. It was sport that helped me develop the perseverance I needed to get up and continue. In cricket, if we heard chin music as the ball whizzed past our ear, we told ourselves that the bowler couldn't bowl a ball that good again and the next ball would be the one that could be despatched to the boundary. In each small failure, I found renewed energy and hope that there was something to look forward to. I was developing the attitude that "the next step has to be good and will be".

The A-ha! moment came near the end of my course at SIBM. We were in the fourth semester and knew how important it was for our future to do well. P C Narayan was our visiting professor and it was his last lecture of the semester and the last lecture for the course. The magic he spun that day changed my life. Narayan asked us to take a piece of paper and write down our life goals using the SMART formula that I will share in a later chapter. When we had written our goals, he told us to keep our papers safe in our wallets. *"Whenever you clean your wallet or handbag, it is time to look at this piece of paper, review it, then fold it, and back it goes in the wallet. The day you achieve your goal, you may tear the paper and celebrate your achievement."* He then went to the blackboard and explained a concept that was so simple and yet is the most powerful secret I have to share with you:

Learning- Prof P C Narayan

The shortest distance between two points is a straight line. If you want to achieve a goal in twenty years that represents happiness for you, you might have milestones to meet every five years. Let's take the case of a marketing student who wants to be a Managing Director by the age of forty-five. At the beginning, you are a management trainee. At the mid-way point, your milestone is to become the Marketing Manager or Vice President of Marketing. Your next milestone is Vice President of Marketing and Sales. If you meet those early milestones, you will be on track to be Managing Director within five years. However, dear reader, life is not this simple.

When we start on the journey we might stray from the straight line between starting point and goal without realising it. When you review your progress along the path, you might find you have strayed from the straight line and need to take corrective action. But when you correct course, inertia can take you off course to the other side of the line. Staying on track to achieve your ultimate goal, means keeping your efforts focused and staying as close as possible on the straight line.

Following Narayan's model of tracking and reviewing helped me more than I had expected. In this book, I share the strategies that kept me close to the straight line and on track to achieve my goals.

Working with the best brands, including Siemens (#1 in Engineering), P&G (#1 in fast-moving consumer goods (FMCG), L'Oréal (#1 in cosmetics and perfumes), and Gillette (#1 in Men's grooming), gave me the experience and belief to build Airtel to the #1 position in Telecom. As the first employee at L'Oréal India, the greenfield project gave me experience and the confidence I needed to build my inner strength to become the Managing Director at Gillette and to later help build an industry at Airtel and *"change the way an average Indian lives"*.

> *I feel blessed that I learnt to build and manage brand at P&G, to build and manage companies at L'Oréal and Gillette, and to build an industry at Airtel.*

Becoming the Managing Director for Gillette in India was not the achievement of the goal I had pursued so relentlessly for decades, but was the beginning of another fulfilling journey that I had not imagined but that unfolded in front of me day by day. During the five and a half years I was with Airtel, the company grew from strength to strength and I was transformed as a leader by external and internal events. Those five years were the golden period of my career. I challenged myself every day and questioned whether the headwinds that I had felt, I was walking into and that had prevented me from progressing, actually existed or were in my head. In the past, my negative thoughts had told me, *I am not good enough, I am not worthy, I am not important, I am helpless, I am not safe*. But at Airtel, I confronted these thoughts. My core beliefs became positive and I was not afraid to challenge myself to transform negative beliefs into awareness.

Building an organisation from nothing to a three million customer base and a more than two-billion-dollar top line, with some of our circles having an EBITDA[1] margin over 60% was an enthralling ride. I was ready to surf and looking for the next big wave. Having worked in Manufacturing, Finance, Marketing and Sales, Distribution, and Logistics and setting up L'Oréal in India, I would have been happy with that level of success and achievement, but my biggest lesson was how much more there was to unlearn and learn.

The fuel to this envious run was my belief in the purpose that made me join Airtel: "change the way the average Indian Lives". My ROI[2] was when some fishermen told me how Airtel had transformed their lives. We had successfully changed the way an average Indian lived. That was when, at the age of fifty, I knew it was time to move on to my next big goal and chase what my heart desired. I had truly moved my Cheese. The next big wave of satisfaction I wanted to surf

---

1   Earnings before Interest, Tax ,Depreciation and Amortisation
2   Return on investment

was to become an executive coach and partner people to transform their lives.

My formal education at Bombay University, SIBM, INSEAD, and further courses at the IIMs, Centre for Creative Leadership (Colorado Springs USA), IMD, SHL, ISB helped shape my career, building organisations in India. Alongside that experience, my coaching journey has been shaped by Results Coaching Systems (David Rock), C4E (TRAC), and Points of You (POY- Israel). It has also developed by attending courses and interacting with world leaders in coaching, including Marshall Goldsmith, Brian Tracy, and Leon Vanderpol, and influenced by the many gurus whom I have learned from and interacted with online, including David Rock, Dr Brene Brown, Dr Deepak Chopra, Judith Glaser, Dr Bruce Lipton, Simon Sinek, and Ram Ramanathan. I am indebted to the International Coach Federation for the rigour they installed in me as a coach, and for their system of continuous educations units (CCEUS) which has made me a learner for life. I am grateful to every member of the ICF Bangalore chapter for challenging me as their President and for our discussions over a cup of tea (Chai pe Charcha).

The satisfaction of having contributed to seeking clarity for a business leader's goal is hard to express or translate into words. Many of the clients I have partnered with have transitioned into a CEO role from a functional CXO. Some A-Ha! moments have been etched into my memory and continue to give me energy and happiness. One leader I worked with wanted to define and express his legacy. It was our third session when the A-ha! moment happened as we worked with POY cards and the realisation helped the leader define his goal with the *feed-forward mechanism* that we will look at later in the book. The first product the leader established for his legacy was project simplicity, which described how the EBITDA of the company could double if executed well.

In another case, I partnered with the leader and one of his senior leaders when they stumbled upon practices in their division that the company did not allow. The issue was serious for them as they were responsible for the operations. The worst-case scenario was that they could lose their jobs, but they decided to display courage and brought the issue to the attention of the Board. In their feedback, the leader and senior leader acknowledged my coaching for giving them the courage and belief to do what their hearts knew was right. They took ownership of their decisions and the consequences. The board was appreciative and took the opportunity to cleanse the system.

For another leader, the coaching dived deep into his strong belief systems that were affecting his behaviour. While he tried to understand where his beliefs emanated from, he also defended them. It took the help of POY to help him think differently. The leader confronted the difficulty of changing beliefs he had held for years. *Do you want to change that? How badly do you wish to see this change?* He was certain he wanted to change but expressed his difficulty. The coin dropped when I asked him, *who is stopping you?* After a prolonged pause, I heard, "*ME*". Transformation had begun. My only response was "*Release the hostage*".

In my journey as a coach, I have realised that a good coach does not try to convince, hence he is convincing. He does not try to influence and that makes him inspiring. A good leader *Acknowledges, Appreciates, Accepts,* and *Allows* what wants to happen.

My Notes

2

FAILURE IS NOT THE OPPOSITE OF SUCCESS, BUT PART OF THE JOURNEY

When you read the chart on the next page, what grabs your attention? Do you see his ultimate success, or do you see the failures that Lincoln experienced and admire his resilience and grit to stay the course? Both perspectives have their merits. Success is a journey and there will be good days and bad days along the way. Every challenge Lincoln faced can be seen as a test to prepare for and be worthy of the chair he wanted to occupy as President of the United States. It was as if life was preparing him for the difficulties of the great responsibility ahead.

1820-26	Worker for hire in neighbour's garden	Daily wage earner
1828	Sister dies giving birth	Personal bereavement
1830	Contests General Assembly elections, Illinois	Loses election
	Business closes down	Near bankruptcy
1842	Marries and has first child	Happiness expressed
1849	Fails to be appointed at the land office	Disappointment
1850	Second child dies at the age of four	Personal bereavement
1851	Father dies	Personal bereavement
1854	Wins election but declines seat, hopes for US Senate	Takes risky decision
1855	Loses US Senate election	Loses election
1859	Loses US Senate election	Loses election
1861	Becomes the 16th President of USA	Achieves the goal

Consider the struggle that Mahatma Gandhi went through. On June 7th, 1893, at a little station called Pietermaritzburg, in South Africa, Gandhi was thrown off a train because of his Indian heritage. It took being thrown off the train for Gandhi to become angry at the discrimination he and others faced every day. Gandhi channelled his anger into the non-violent protest movement that has changed the world. I remember my father telling me that each one of us has our struggles and stories to write. Resilience and success are about learning to *acknowledge, accept,* and *appreciate* everything that happens in our lives, good and bad. Every setback has a lesson to offer. Are we ready to learn?

"I hated every minute of training, but I said, don't quit. Suffer now and live the rest of your life as a champion."

— MUHAMMAD ALI

Patience Pays

Many of us are ready to give up on our dreams when we are on the home stretch. We may be only a yard away from success and yet we give up. But it may be too early to quit. And when I say quit, I mean move the goalposts. Many executives are too ready to move the goalposts rather than persist for success. Every one of us has put in an enormous amount to be where we are and have been authentic in our effort and persistence to reach this far. We need to trust and believe that we all go through difficult phases in life but are born to conquer.

When Geoff Skingsley took charge as the first CEO for L'Oréal India, I knew that if I was to be the next CEO I would have to wait at least five more years. I debated with myself about whether I should persist and had convinced myself that, since I was enjoying my current job and the journey to my goal, I should be ok with not being a CEO by the age of forty. But during this period of introspection, I asked myself, why didn't I believe that I could become CEO of another company by forty and enjoy it just as much? In this way, my disappointment allowed me to challenge a limiting belief that a CEO must be groomed from within the organisation.

Along the journey to our goals, we may need to take stock, rewind a bit and re-boot if necessary, and re-think our strategies, to carry on with extra energy. You will conquer your fears, you will conquer your limiting beliefs and set yourself free. To start, all we need is an open mind and a willingness to move out of our comfort zone.

In this chapter, I will introduce some principles that we will explore more deeply in the following chapters. This book will help you focus on what is critical for you to achieve your goal. It will help you to have the courage to hear your voice, make you strong enough to listen to your heart, and bold enough to live the life you want.

When we are on the verge of giving up, what state of mind are we in?

Some of the thoughts our minds may process include:
- *Everybody is against me.*
- *My team members are on their own trip, they are simply not aligned.*
- *I don't know why they don't see it as clearly as I do.*
- *This system doesn't deserve a person of my caliber.*
- *That promotion should have been mine, I just can't be a yes person.*
- *I don't have a godfather to look after my career.*
- *My boss and I just don't seem to agree on most matters. I think he doesn't like me.*

What do you feel when you are in this state of mind?
(Circle the words below, or add your own)

Afraid   Abandoned   Angry   Annoyed   Anxious

Confused   Depressed   Desperate   Embarrassed Frustrated   Helpless

Hopeless   Hurt   Impatient   Insecure   Invisible   Jealous

Nervous   Rejected   Tense   Upset   Worried

FAILURE IS NOT THE OPPOSITE OF SUCCESS, BUT PART OF THE JOURNEY

How do you act when you are in this state of mind?
(Circle the phrases below, or add your own)

Argue to prove your point   Belittle others   Blame others

Bully juniors   Complain and crib about every small thing

Cry   Drink, eat or smoke more than usual

Avoid difficult situations   Fight unnecessarily

Find fault with everybody and everything

Give up on people and situations   Gossip and spread rumours

Insult people   Interrupt when others are speaking and not listen

Lose sleep   Self-pity

Manipulate data and people   Become resentful

Preach Pretend   Procrastinate.

That is when we need to pause. Ask yourself:

1. What knowledge is it that I am missing here?
2. What is it that I am not seeing here?
3. How could I see this differently?
4. How can I grow from this?

5. What is it that I need to pay attention to now?
6. What is it that wants to happen?
7. What is the opportunity for me?

> If you live long enough, you'll make mistakes. But if you learn from them, you'll be a better person. It's how you handle adversity, not how it affects you. The main thing is never quit, never quit, never quit
>
> — WILLIAM J. CLINTON

Keep it simple – the rule of three

In life, there are only three things in our control: our perceptions, our decisions, and our actions. Likewise, in a career, there are only three things to focus on: the self, the team, and the system. To understand any issue in your career and keep moving forward, the first step is to break down the issue into these three aspects of self, team, and the system.

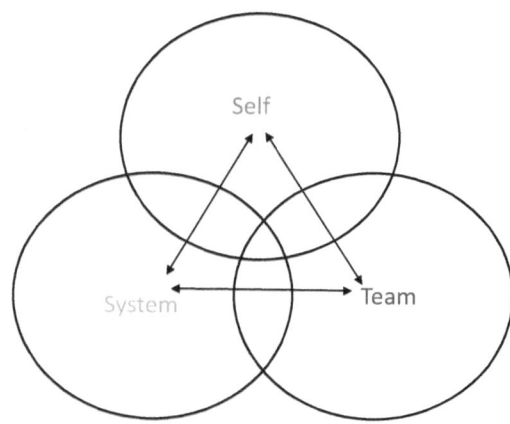

Just as being customer-centric means attending to people, processes, and strategic inputs, being employee centric means seeing issues through the lens of the self, the team, and the system. We need to understand the impact we have on our team and the system, and the impact the team and the system have on us. Most of our time should be devoted to focusing on the self to understand the impact and influence of our own beliefs and actions, but we tend to do the opposite and focus instead on the external aspects of the issue: teams and systems. When we focus on the external rather than listening to ourselves, we get ahead of ourselves and try to control teams and systems, which is futile. At best, we can influence teams and systems through our communication, behaviour, and actions.

We have control over only three things in our lives: our perceptions, our decisions, and our actions

Our Perceptions. *Others' perceptions of me will change when my perception of myself changes.* There will always be a lag between these two events as others' perception of me is based on my past behaviour, and my perception of myself is based on how I see myself in the future.

Our Decisions. This is the first step to action. We make decisions throughout our lives and there has been much research about decision-making. We are always trying to understand how we make decisions and how we can make better decisions. Researchers and scholars have developed models to help us make better decisions. The 2x2 matrix for urgent vs important tasks helps us decide which tasks to delegate, which tasks to defer, and which tasks need immediate attention. SWOT analysis is another example of a 2x2 matrix that helps us to analyse challenges based on our strengths and weaknesses and the opportunities and threats of the challenge.

Our Actions. The most difficult action to take is to step outside our comfort zone. Taking action is all about taking the first step towards your goal and the rest will follow. We do not address our fears when we act but before we take that first step. Addressing your fears will help you to act. In many situations, sharing your vulnerabilities will also help you to act. Taking action then leads to further insights and learning.

So, how do we control these things?

Self-awareness leads to insight

When I was at Airtel I experienced rappelling for the first time during a team-building exercise with Pegasus. It was about overcoming fear. I found myself looking down a sheer, seventy-foot, overhanging rock face, utterly terrified. But I learnt more than just overcoming my fear in that moment. To overcome that fear I had to surrender to it, and that was freedom. Take the first step and be vulnerable to overcome the fear that is stopping you.

The second thing I learnt was that there was enough within my control to take care of myself. What was in my control was to be calm, to believe in the person who held the rope, to understand how the rappel brake worked, to test it out initially, to take one step at a time, to believe in myself, and, of course, to have fun.

By the end of the rappelling exercise, I had some questions for myself:
Do I know what can I control in my life?
1. Am I a secure base to my team, and am I worthy of implicit faith and trust?

2. How do I build such trust?
3. Do I understand vulnerability? Is vulnerability a weakness?
4. In team dynamics, what are the levers of productivity and who pushes them?
5. The team was watching my every step, what if I had panicked?
6. Was I able to influence and motivate some of my team members?
7. Did I put myself at risk, or was it just another process?

Vulnerability is a sign of self-belief

You need to decode your mindset and understand your patterns of thought. Ask a group of friends or your team members how they would define success, authenticity, or focus. Ask yourself, how do you gain clarity? What are your sources of power? How do you visualise potential and how would you explore your full potential?

Every one of us needs the propulsion in our lives and careers that comes from self-belief but if we are not willing to be vulnerable, self-knowledge and self-belief will be incomplete. Many of us were taught during our childhood that vulnerability is a bad word. So, how can we turn it into a strength? Is it possible? The answer is, that you embrace your vulnerability only when you express it. Being willing to be vulnerable is about communicating your transparency. If we refuse the opportunity to be vulnerable and face our fears, we hold ourselves hostage and become the biggest hurdle to our progress.

Communication binds us

Communication is key. It is the leader's job to open up possibilities for their team, and when a vision is clear it is easy to act on. A leader's vision can become clear through communication. If you stop communicating the vision, it will soon disappear from your team's sight. Therefore, a leader must communicate effectively and precisely.

To communicate effectively and be understood, we first need to listen for understanding – ourselves and our teams. Are you aware of how your communication quotient (CQ) is affecting your intelligence quotient (IQ), emotional quotient (EQ), and spiritual quotient (SQ)? The way you communicate with yourself can create limiting beliefs that later become habits that impede our progress in ways that we are not aware of. Are you aware of how your team is receiving your communication? Leaders are expected to coach their team members. Would you like to be the two-minute coach to your team?

What struck me during a short course with Isabelle Hasleder, the "horse leadership coach", was that a horse responds to the rider's emotions and how the rider handles their own emotions. Communication with a horse is essential for managing the horse's behaviour. The horse's comfort level with the rider's communication decides whether it will take the next step. If a horse must be led through an obstacle course, the rider's belief in the horse and how it is communicated is paramount for successfully clearing the obstacles. If the rider tries to force the horse, the horse will show resentment. If the rider wants the horse to trot majestically, the rider must expect the horse to trot as a response to their belief, their management of their emotions, and their actions. My experience in this course, and many other experiences, have strengthened my belief that we need to look within ourselves to effectively manage issues that are outside of ourselves. Self-awareness and communication are very important tools in a leader's kit bag. Do you sharpen your tools regularly to excel in the game called leadership?

Slow down to gain speed

When you focus on yourself, stay present, and observe your behaviour and what you express from other people's points of view, you develop self-awareness. Self-awareness involves becoming aware of multiple aspects of your being: your traits, likes and dislikes, behaviours, feelings, and how you express them. If you can reflect on your personality and character and consider how others may perceive your character, your journey to self-awareness has begun. Just as you see patterns in others' behaviour, can you see patterns in your own behaviour? With greater self-awareness, we also experience greater emotional, behavioural and cognitive development.

Thoughts and emotions can intervene and disturb the space between you and the place, person, or thing you are with. Even when you are alone, these disturbances can happen and separate us from those we need to communicate with. To keep this space sacred, we need to focus and be present and aware in the moment. This may involve slowing down to the *Speed of Presence*. When we are at the speed of presence we are at our productive best. We will find out more about the speed of presence in the coming chapters.

Trust is a bonding agent

Trust is the foundation on which success stories are built. It is from trust that dreams become a reality: trust in yourself, trust in your potential, and trust in pushing your limits to find new boundaries. Nothing can be achieved alone – we all need to work with people to achieve our dreams. Our brains are designed for connection and all our behaviours and strategies are aligned to this simple biological truth. We need people, but how do we build trust? And whose responsibility is it to build trust? Who is the owner of this process, what is the starting point, and is there a framework?

These reflections may make you want to change some of your habits, and wonder whether it is possible to move away from old habits and create new ones. Creating new habits is possible for all of us. We may first ask, how should I go about changing my habits and can I trust myself to do this?

So, what do we do with this awareness? How does this help me to be more productive? How do I use this to influence my team members? How do I have more impact with my communication and influence my team into action? Here, your most productive, creative self, your true self, needs to come to the fore. This is when you experience the speed of presence. The speed of presence is just one of the ingredients that will help you build an executive presence that will be felt even in your absence.

Through this book, I aim to help you through the maze, clear away the cobwebs, and clarify your thoughts. You can get back to the straight line, the shortest route from where you are now to where you want to be. Research tells us that *people are willing to change only when the risk of maintaining the status quo is perceived to be greater than the risk of change*. This is why over 80% of people stay in their comfort zones.

If you want to see a change in your team members, you must first ask yourself if you are willing to change. How much are you willing to risk?

This book will help you to see both positive and limiting thoughts in their true light. Limiting beliefs and behaviour patterns will hold you back. They are the headwinds that slow your progress down, hold you and your team hostage, and prevent you from taking action.

In the next chapter, we turn to our *potential* and consider what we need to know and do to experience our full potential. As you read, I hope that my experiences will help motivate you into action to make your map for the future more meaningful than an image in your mind.

My Notes

3

UNLEASH YOUR POTENTIAL

"The only person you are destined to become is the person you decide to be."

— Ralph Waldo Emerson

Are you living up to your full potential? I kept asking myself this question. I think I stopped asking when I was appointed Managing Director for Gillette. My friend Sanjay Banerjee commented that I had not yet done justice to my potential, and I agree that you can limit your growth and potential by simply not dreaming big enough. This thought was reiterated by another friend, A R Menon. Our potential is our capacity to develop in the future, and this capacity transcends our specific goals to connect with our bigger purpose in life. When I joined Gillette, I had a goal, but it was purpose that later drove me to join Airtel. However, having the capacity to develop is no guarantee that you will – many a brilliant idea has stayed on the drawing board.

Our potential is made up of our strengths, capabilities, and aspirations. The bigger we dream, the more we will need to push the limits of our potential to achieve our goals. Pushing these limits involves a willingness to innovate and reinvent ourselves. We need to be fully aware of what is stopping us, what our limiting beliefs are, and where they come from. Are we holding ourselves back as a hostage to fear? Are we ready to face our fears? Are my limiting beliefs the reason I feel helpless and paralysed at times? People often ask, "Where do I begin?" Let's start with what is in our control: *the rule of three.*

Focus on what you can control

As I mentioned in the last chapter, there are only three things in our lives that are within our control:
1. Our Perceptions
2. Our Decisions
3. Our Actions

Nothing else is within our control. Let's explore this at a deeper level.

Perceptions

Perceptions are real, even if they do not correspond directly to reality. Everything is in the mind of the holder. When you see a piece of art there are many possible perceptions and interpretations of that piece.

In the same way, everyone has their own perceptions of others. While each person's perceptions are true for them, they may be completely different from another person's perceptions. These differences arise from the different experiences people have of others and over their lifetimes.

> *Your perception of yourself is what helps you define your potential.*

We can't control other people's perceptions of us. So, should we allow other people's perceptions to define us? Or should we take Angelina Jolie's approach: "If I make a fool of myself, who cares? I'm not frightened by anyone's perception of me." There may be an element of truth in others' perceptions, so it is prudent to consider their perspectives and take on this feedback. Right or wrong, the reality is that others' perceptions influence our beliefs, our behaviour, and the way we communicate. The way you interpreted Abraham Lincoln's life story or Muhammad Ali's statement depended on your past perceptions and experiences.

> *Perceptions depend on three things: attention, retention, and distortion.*

1. Attention. When you meet someone for the first time, what do you pay attention to? If you believe that it's important to dress well, you'll pay attention to what they are wearing. If you believe that it's important to communicate well, you'll pay attention to how they communicate. If a smile signals a pleasing personality to you, then you'll pay attention to this trait. What you pay attention to is what you use to create your mental image of that person, and your future interactions with that person will reinforce or revise your mental image of them. *Your experiences with the person make your perceptions of that person.*

The same thing is true for events and situations. If you witness an accident, your past experiences and your knowledge and interpretation of shared rules and conventions will determine how you understand the causes and effects of the accident. Events don't directly produce our understandings – how we perceive them matters. But our perceptions can be biased. When our perceptions are skewed by inaccurate beliefs and past experiences, our understandings may stray further from reality and further from understandings that are shared with others.

For many years I believed that obese people lacked willpower. This bias was not based on evidence and it hampered my recruitment mindset until I recognised my bias and consciously dropped it. Most of us are unaware of our biases and they become habitual ways of thinking that we use to judge others.

2. **Retention.** After any incident, your perceptions and interpretations are registered and retained in memory and are available for later recall. Memories can be lost when retention fails. They can also change over time, such as when discussing the memory with others and their perspectives influence what we remember. In this way, fresh perceptions can change others' mental image of you, such as the new impressions being formed when you interact with your boss or a colleague. *While language has an impact, what others retain most is how you make them feel.* In most human transactions, the effect of your behaviour on other people's emotions is far more important than what you say.

3. **Distortion.** Let's say that you're meeting a person at an inter-departmental meeting. The last time you met this person in the

corridors of the office, they were annoyed and asked you to please stop asking their team members questions about the status of their project as it will be delivered as per the agreed schedule. Ask yourself, is that episode still hurting you? Will it colour your perceptions of what this person says in the meeting? We all see others through coloured glasses. *Are you carrying baggage on your journey to reaching your full potential?*

Decisions

Decisions are the choices we make. We have been making decisions since childhood. Parents might believe that they are the ones who make the choices, but just ask the child! As adults, we like to believe we make decisions through an active, reasoned process of selection from options available based on their merits. However, decision-making is also critically influenced by the perceptions, values, preferences, and beliefs of the decision-maker. While decision-making is a cognitive process, it is not always a conscious process that we are aware of or that we control. Do you think before every action you take? If we did, perhaps we would be aware of the unconscious beliefs and perceptions that hold us back.

Do you decide when to get angry?

Do you decide when to yell when you are under stress?

When you spoke ill of someone, was it a reasoned choice?

When you respond to fear of the unknown, is your choice always reasonable?

When you pass judgement on others, is it based on conscious choices?

When a habit takes over, you are no longer in control of your cognitive decision-making processes. The brain uses your senses and perceptions, shaped by experience and biases, to map your current situation. Actions are initiated automatically based on how you have responded in similar situations in the past. The habit kicks in automatically and involuntarily. When you want to take control of a habit, you have decided to change the habit. Neuroplasticity confirms that you can. It is possible to exercise control and interrupt automatic decision-making processes to resist behaving out of habit.

Decision-making is more than a cognitive process. Let me explain...

We can think of our nervous system as three "brains": the *cephalic brain*, the *cardiac brain*, and the *enteric brain*. These "brains" are neural networks of brain cells that process information from inside and outside of the body. Let's appreciate some commons statements and how they relate to the three "brains":

Let me get my head into this. She has a head for this kind of stuff. Has he lost his head? Keep your head above water Running around like a headless chicken. Use your head	**Mind intelligence/Cephalic brain** 50 to 100 billion neurons Function: Cognitive, Perceptions Thinking, making meaning
Head vs Heart Wears his heart on his sleeve Close to my heart Disheartened Straight to the heart Heavy/light-hearted	**Heart Intelligence/Cardiac brain** 30 to 120 thousand neurons Function: Emotive, Valuing Relational affect
Gut instinct/response Go with your gut, trust it Hard to swallow My stomach was tied up in knots No guts, no glory Take some time to digest it	**Gut Intelligence/Enteric Brain** 200 to 500 million neurons Function: Identity, mobilisation Self-preservation

When you look at the functions of each of these neural networks, it is clear that all three have a role to play. Yet we rarely use all three when we make a decision. Ideally, decision-making would start in the cardiac "brain", which would send the issue to the cephalic "brain" to collect as much data as possible, which would then send the data back to the cardiac brain for further processing. This processed data would then be sent to the enteric "brain" to gather further data and be processed further before being sent back to the cardiac brain. This loop would continue processing the available information until the individual is satisfied and accepts the solution. While we think we make reasoned decisions based on data from the cephalic brain, in reality we often make decisions without conscious awareness of the influence of our emotions, perceptions, and experience. If we do attempt to listen to the enteric brain, the debate between the enteric and the cephalic brain is so loud that the feeble voice of the heart is drowned.

Actions

If you have ever given a TV interview, the words, "Camera, rolling, action," will be familiar. If you have played competitive cricket and were the opening batsman, ready to face the first ball of the match, you would have heard the umpire say, "Play." If you have been into athletics, the words, "On your mark, set, go", will be familiar. These are action words that trigger you into action.

Let's take the example of sky diving. You may have read about the thrill of sky diving, the exhilaration as your adrenalin pumps. It's the thrill you have always sought but experienced only in small doses. Your perception of the excitement of sky diving and your desire to experience new things may have put it high on your wish list. You've read about the dangers and spoken to friends who have experienced it but when you are on the plane before sky diving for the first time after all your preparation, just before you jump you feel butterflies in your stomach. The butterflies are your enteric brain cautioning you and playing its role in self-preservation. Action is that step you take off the plane at twenty thousand feet above sea level when you conquer your fears and let go. Without action, our mental map of the potential future remains a mental image. What's your action word? My mantra is, "When in doubt, do it." This mantra helped me join the dots to achieve the future I imagined.

> "Continuous effort—not strength or intelligence—
> is the key to unlocking our potential."
>
> — WINSTON CHURCHILL

Dive deep to test your potential

To test your potential, you need to dive deep and test the depths and take the currents against you in your stride with gratitude, along with more favourable currents. Without action, you will never know the direction to take or the changes and disruptions you may need to orchestrate in your journey. The journey to full potential is one of faith and belief and it's your belief in your potential that will help you join the dots in the future. It's your self-belief that will help you build strategies and carve a path to take forward. Others may tell you that your chosen course of action is not the right thing to do. But that's their opinion and you have a

responsibility to yourself. I won't say don't listen to others, but take your own decisions, and make them decisions you believe in. To enjoy the journey, keep it simple and focus on three simple attitudes:
1. Be inspired
2. Be abundant
3. Be in service

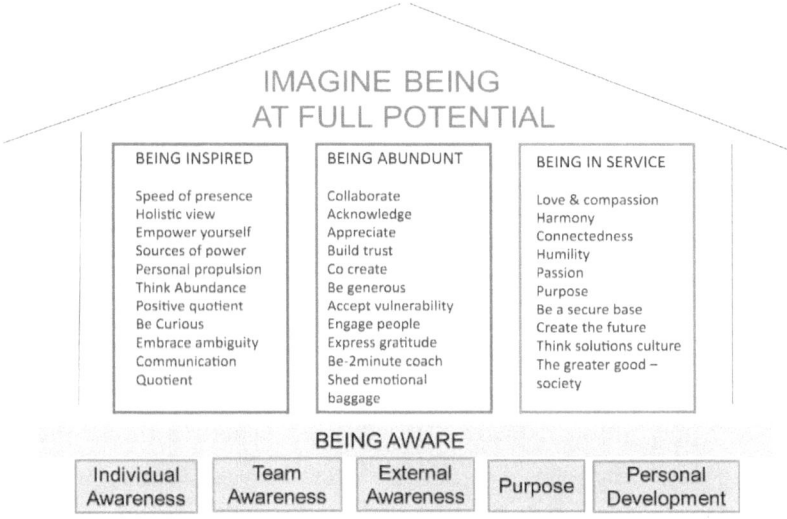

Being inspired

We all look for role models and inspirational stories to help us move forward. Yes, these stories are important as they give us perspective and may help trigger our innate desire to challenge the status quo. On this long journey, if there is one person who can be with you through thick and thin, constantly by your side, it is yourself. You must be inspired by your own thoughts and deeds.

To inspire yourself daily and understand your strengths and capabilities, you need to slow down to gain speed. Try to decipher your sources of power and how to use that power. Move consciously to being accountable for your behaviour, rather than finding fault elsewhere and blaming others. Understand from simple aerodynamics that the more emotional baggage you carry from the past, the slower you will move forward. Perhaps the most important ingredient for inspiring yourself is to understand and learn *the right way to communicate with yourself*. This is where many people stall and where you may be your own worst enemy.

Being abundant

It was at the Centre for Creative Leadership (CCL) at Colorado Springs that the phenomenon of abundance dawned on me and it has continued to have a deep impact on my life. There, I began to understand the meaning of abundance at a deeper level. It was as though the tree outside the window of our meeting room was talking to me and explaining how people need to learn from nature and remember that we are part of the natures' cycle and must act responsibly. We need to be as vulnerable and generous as nature. There will be enough for everyone if we learn to share and live in harmony.

> *Acknowledge, appreciate, accept, and allow events in life to take place.*

Count your blessings. When you are grateful for the small things in life your blessings will grow. If you chase wealth, I am not sure it will ever come. But if you are grateful for what you have, you will see it grow. If you are grateful for the job you have, even if it is not your dream job, you will see it transform into your dream job. Something I learnt from Sam, my driver at Airtel, was that if we don't count our blessings, we may fall into the trap of counting the negatives. Our attention will move from the positives of life to the negatives, and the more we attend to the negative, the more negatives we will perceive. This cycle depletes the positive energy in our system and may begin to detract from our blessings. The practice of counting your blessings is so simple and yet so powerful that it will change your life.

The more gratitude you feel, the happier you will be. Try it.

Being in service

Being in service to others helps us to inspire and be abundant in our approach. When you inspire yourself, you are in a state of abundance and this will help you to adopt an attitude of service. Is it possible to see all people you interact with as complete and capable individuals? If you accept the idea that everyone can be complete, you will begin to think, "How can I serve?" rather than, "how do I take advantage of the situation?" You will not ask, "What's in it for me"? Instead, you will foster powerful connections that will lead to deep relationships.

There seems to be a very powerful connection between being in service and finding your purpose. When I adopted the attitude of being in service, I grew many times over as a person and this growth was reflected in my company's growth in revenue and EBITDA. I saw my team transform into a well-knit unit that was ready to conquer the world.

If you look at the diagram at the beginning of this chapter, "Imagine being your full potential", you will see that the foundation to this journey is awareness. Awareness is an amazing journey in itself. The more aware you become, the more there is to be aware of. It is a never-ending journey of fulfilment. We'll explore more about how to become aware in the chapters ahead.

> *To live a wholehearted life and ensure you achieve your goals, you need to be inspired, be abundant and be in service.*

Join me on this journey to explore your potential. Are you ready? Are you ready to *release the hostage*?

4

CREATE AWARENESS, IT IS THE FOUNDATION

"The first step towards change is awareness, the second step is acceptance."

— Nathaniel Branden

Awareness is the foundation to full potential

Have you ever questioned your beliefs or thoughts? What makes every one of us unique in the way we think? What makes our thinking patterns different?

People have been asking questions since ancient times. Siddhartha Goutam (Gautam Buddha) looked for answers in the collective wisdom of the past and from wise people around him. His constant questioning had him thinking along with others. When he didn't find answers that satisfied him, he looked inward. He took his awareness to a level rarely seen. Some people refer to this capability of the mind as a supernatural power. Did he get into an intellectual analysis? To me, Siddhartha Goutam saw reality as it was, having freed himself from bias through introspection. He had truly centred himself.

Awareness helps us make choices that lead to results. Every time you find yourself confused, be curious, be very curious. This chapter will help you develop the skills to be more aware of yourself. Gandhi's words will help you start your journey to self-awareness:

> Your beliefs become your thoughts
> Your thoughts become your words
> Your words become your actions
> Your actions become your habits
> Your habits become your values
> Your values become your destiny
>
> — MAHATMA GANDHI

Be curious

Remember, as children, we were full of curiosity. We wanted to understand everything our parents did or didn't allow us to do. We asked open-ended questions and followed them with deep, penetrating, searching questions.

Ask questions to gain awareness of different aspects of your being: your traits, likes and dislikes, behaviours, feelings and how you express your emotions. When you focus on yourself and observe your behaviours

CREATE AWARENESS, IT IS THE FOUNDATION

and others' perceptions of you from outside yourself, you will learn the art of self-awareness. If you can reflect on your personality and the impression you make on other people, your journey to self-awareness has begun. Just as you see patterns in others' behaviour, you can see patterns in your behaviour. When self-awareness is high, we begin to attend to our emotional and behavioural development as well as our cognitive development.

We don't see things the way they are, we see things the way we are. What does this mean? It simply means that the ways we think, analyse, interact, and behave, strongly shape our perceptions of the world around us, other people, events, and ourselves. We can only see things through the lens of our own beliefs and experiences. Our beliefs, including our limiting beliefs, our rules, our view of the world, play a major role in the way we are.

Patterns are what we do repeatedly: *he is always late to meetings, she is so accident-prone, she changes her job every two years*. These statements describe patterns that can become habits. To change your life, change your habits. The way we think is one of these habits.

Are you aware of your patterns of thinking? Sometimes hypothetical questions can open us up to insight:

1. If you were offered Rs 1000.00 for eating live worms, would you?
2. If you were in a hurry and wanted to beat the traffic, would you take a shortcut through a "no entry" street?
3. When you were reversing your car, you scratched a brand new BMW in the car park. You are sure no one has seen you. Would you leave your name and number?
4. If by killing one person you could feed all the hungry people in the world, would you?

Hypothetical questions like these can help you understand your patterns. Go ahead and try to understand your model of how you learn. Put it on paper. What are your patterns of communication?

Personal awareness questions

A very good starting point in your journey to self-awareness is to develop the habit of curiosity. Curiosity is directly related to being open to personal growth and the ability to connect with others. Curiosity helps us to think deeper and this enhances our cognitive capacity. Curiosity also helps us adjust to new experiences and be comfortable in the grey zones of our lives.

Curiosity is also a great tool to demonstrate and convey empathy – ask open-ended questions, be curious about yourself. The questions below are a great start:

1. Is my behaviour causing my team to be dysfunctional?
2. When I communicate, am I reaching my team members?
3. When I communicate, am I precise and easy to understand?
4. What makes me happy? What makes me sad?
5. What triggers my anger?
6. Am I empathetic enough? How do I demonstrate empathy?
7. Do I need to better express or demonstrate my love and compassion?
8. If there is one thing that I need to change in my life, what is it?
9. What do I need to stop doing now?

Go ahead and write some questions to ask yourself.

On this journey to self-awareness, we need structure and some help from a buddy. Have a buddy coach, or simply ask your pillow to be your buddy coach! A buddy coach will help you introspect every day. Every night, your pillow needs to ask you the daily questions listed below.

Questions for daily reflection

1. Have you done enough or done your best to be happy?
2. Have you done enough or done your best to move towards your goal?
3. Have you done enough or done your best to communicate clearly?
4. Have you done enough or done your best to influence your team members?

Go ahead and write your questions to ask every day.

Asking yourself questions that make you think and reflect needs to become a routine practice. Just as you review your team's performance, you need to regularly reflect on your journey and the progress you've made.

> *The quality of the questions you ask yourself determines the quality of the life you lead*

Awareness leads to choices

At the core of awareness is how we present ourselves. Some of the people I have coached believed they should behave differently in different roles. However, the ideal state is where roles are not important and instead the different aspects of a person are aligned within their whole self. Then, we can be our most authentic selves.

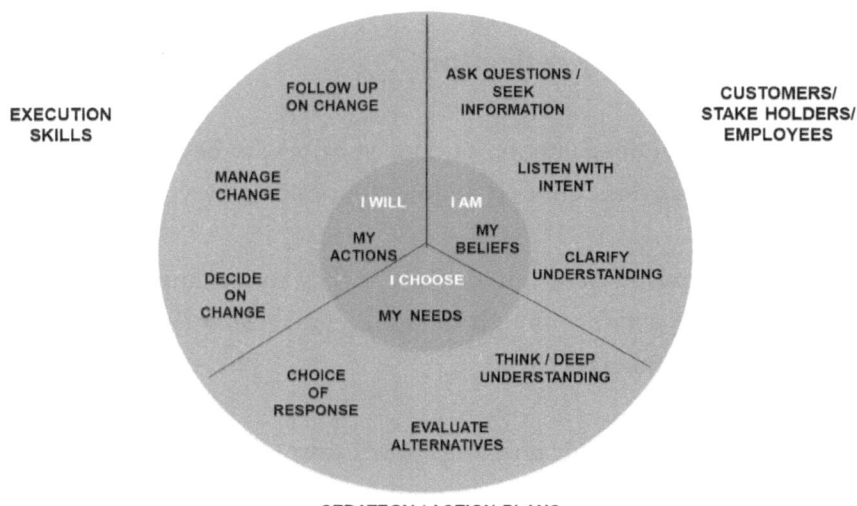

When asked whether they are aware of their beliefs, most people answer that they are. Have you ever written down your belief statements? Go ahead and write them down now and believe in the impact they will have on you and your life.

Some of my belief statements are:
- Every person has a coach within.
- To be in the moment I have to surrender myself.
- A person changes only when they decide to change.
- My failures are what I have achieved – they have not come automatically.

Who am I?

Write down 10 or more statements beginning with "I am…"
For example:
- I am an inspirational leader.
- I am what I am because of my choices in the past and this gives me the power to create the future I want.

Aim to go beyond simple descriptive statements of your behaviour such as, "I am honest", "I am punctual", etc. Think deeply and aim to define your being.

My needs influence my choices

My needs are what I make of them, and my choices are the decisions I have made. The needs we experience are varied, but we can classify them:
- Need for status – the status I refer to here is the status within us, a good feeling.
- Need for security – the feeling of being secure and able to take care of my family.
- Need for growth – including different kinds of growth, such as knowledge, wealth, skills, and mental agility.
- Need for love and compassion
- Need to be engaged
- Need to contribute
- Need for materialistic comforts
- Need for an identity

Go ahead and write down your needs and try to define each one.

To think more deeply about needs, classify your needs in three columns: *What I need a lot of, what I need more of, and what would be nice to have.* For example, I need to own a jet plane (nice to have). This exercise will help you to understand what comes naturally and what requires focus and effort to satisfy. Some needs might make you feel good but may not have your focus.

Need a lot of...	Need more of...	Nice to have...

Write down ten or more statements beginning with "I choose…" These statements should flow from the needs you have written down, and you will begin to make the connections. You may want to update your answers if you find your needs are misaligned with your choices:

- I choose to always be on the right side of the law.
- I choose the people I wish to spend time with.
- I choose what I want to do and this helps me make time for myself.

When in doubt, do it

Action orientation is very important. Only action will reinforce your beliefs and empower you to push the limits of your potential. A bias for action should be high on your list of priorities.

- Execution is critical for any strategy to succeed.
- Execution is a discipline and a critical component of your transformation.

- You are responsible for action and it cannot be outsourced or delegated.
- A bias for action needs to be close to your core, your authentic self.
- Positive action is taken when your cardiac brain, enteric brain, and cephalic brain are aligned. This will happen only when there is a robust dialogue between the three networks.

Go ahead and define what action means to you and how you would describe your actions:
1. My actions are thought through.
2. My actions are fair and just to all those who are affected by them.
3. My actions are flexible in response to feedback and lead indicators.

Write down ten or more statements beginning with "I will…" These statements will push you into action mode:
- I will take complete ownership of the consequences of my actions.
- I will acknowledge, appreciate, accept and allow events in my life to happen.
- I will always be on time.
- I will accept disruption as part of learning and growing.

The statements that prompt you into action are critical. The statements and beliefs that drive you into action mode with confidence and self-belief are what we will call *power codes*. Power codes can assist you in your daily life. These statements are close to your belief statements

and are on a higher plane than action statements. Some examples will help demonstrate what power codes are. Some of my power codes are:
1. Vision, purpose, and goals are bigger than the moment.
2. I set benchmarks for every event.
3. I create powerful experiences.
4. Words create pictures in my brain.
5. I am the master of my destiny.

Go ahead and write your power codes.

> "Believe nothing, no matter where you read it, or who said it, no matter if I have said it, unless it agrees with your own reason and your own common sense."
>
> — BUDDHA.

Self-awareness is a skill

Research has shown that humans have a range of unconscious biases. Daniel Kahneman described how, despite us believing we know ourselves, we are frequently wrong. Some research has found that Indian managers who match up to their international counterparts in almost all aspects, fall short when it comes to self-awareness. It turns out, we are not as self-aware as we think we are. Like any other skill, the development of self-awareness is achieved in stages from unconscious incompetence to unconscious competence.

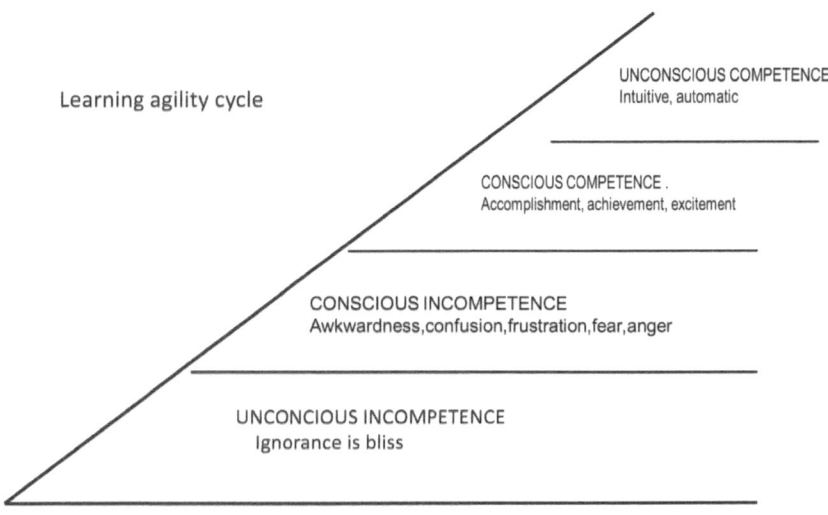

How would you work your way through building a habit.
e.g. Leadership skills – Influence/ Executive presence/ Level 3 communication

Daniel Goleman's work on emotional intelligence is insightful. The core of emotional intelligence is self-awareness and self-management. If you can improve your self-awareness and self-management, you will find tremendous corresponding improvement in your management of relationships and your productivity. Leadership potential is leveraged through these core areas. Look at the successful leaders in the world, or look closer to home at the role models you are hoping to emulate: exceptional leaders stand tall because of their self-leadership.

My self-awareness has helped me realise that, while I may not be a deep thinker, I am certainly a deep believer. As a deep believer, my actions lead me to introspection and this has led me to self-leadership.

Self-leadership is a reflection of awareness

Self-leadership is a rare skill. What makes self-leadership so difficult? I believe it is because self-leadership is not a feature of the dominant leadership methods in today's corporate and political world.

The first seven years of our lives are crucial. In those years, we are in the phase of unconscious incompetence and are easily impressed with the outside world. We believe that what we see and want to emulate is the conscious reality. In this phase, our environment seems conventional to us in its rules and behaviour. We don't see people's rules and behaviour as conscious incompetence until much later in life. But while the outer conventional world is structured and has order, our inner core is chaotic. There is so much confusion inside us that we prefer the structure and order we perceive outside. It is easier to sink into the materialistic world and be in harmony with the outside so that we can find harmony within. Everything we don't yet know, or fail to observe within ourselves, is outside what we are conscious of and, therefore, unconscious and a kind of bliss.

In the first half of our lives, we use different sources of power to build an identity. Our identities support a healthy ego, which takes over our lives as we become successful in the outside world's structure and order. It is in the second half of our lives that we tend to look inward, as Jung described.

Self-leadership is observing and managing yourself and taking responsibility for your actions and behaviours. When you achieve self-leadership, you stop looking for approval and projecting authority onto others. On your path to self-leadership, you will find yourself developing qualities of honesty, discipline, humility, love, compassion, accountability, courage, curiosity, assertiveness, and self-belief. Your self-leadership will have an impact on the people around you.

Awareness defines ethics

The main focus of our education system has been on cognitive development, with our emotional and behavioural development left in the hands of our friends, family, and society. We model our behaviour on what is valued in our culture, and our culture defines success as the fulfilment of materialistic needs. Wall Street and Dalal Street glorify CEOs who have done well in the business world. But while we marvel at their business achievements, a few of these individuals have loosely held values. A culture that accepts the unacceptable is not a culture of self-leadership and responsibility.

Exposure aids awareness

As a young boy, I visited my grandparents every year in their village and had many fascinating experiences. I travelled with them in their rural sales van and learnt the nuances of sales. At their printing press, I learnt the printing process and the art of binding school books. In the general store, I saw how important it was for my grandfather to maintain and invest in relationships. In the truck hired to bring in material for the villagers, I travelled and learned about the topography and culture of rural India.

It was on one of those holidays at Moodbidri when I was 14 years old that my cousin, Ashok, and I decided to take the truck for a spin. The truck driver was asleep and we took the keys and started the truck. Ashok was at the wheel first and then I took over. Unfortunately for me, when we passed my grandfather out on his evening walk, it was me he saw behind the wheel. When we got back later that evening, he gave me a stern piece of his mind in a voice so low it was hardly audible. I knew this was serious stuff as I had never heard my grandfather speak so seriously before. It left a lasting impression when he said, "You are an intelligent kid, how could you put the lives of others at risk?" *What an attitude, Grandpa!* It was my first lesson in taking ownership of the choices I made. It was my first lesson in self-awareness and I began to take this journey very seriously.

On this journey to self-awareness and self-leadership, questions that have come to me time and time again will come to you:

1. What is my purpose or vision?
2. What is my long-term goal?
3. Am I on track to achieve my goal?
4. What should my next step be?

When you complete the exercises in this chapter, you will have a lot of information to work on. Every piece of this information is important to *release the hostage* in you.

- Classify your answers to the exercises into three groups: *what you need to continue doing, what you need to do more of, and what you need to stop doing.*
- Evaluate your answers and arrange them in order of priority within the three groups.
- Then, for each priority, write a goal statement that is SMART, PURE, and CLEAR

Smart goals are *Specific, Measurable, Agreed upon, Realistic, and Time-bound*:

SMART	PURE	CLEAR
Specific	Positively stated	Challenging
Measurable	Understood	Legal
Agreed upon	Relevant	Environmentally sound
Realistic	Ethical	Attainable
Timebound		Recorded for measurement

Your goal statements should specify the behaviour you want to display. The goal should be stated as positive behaviour you want to demonstrate, rather than a negative behaviour to avoid. The brain does not understand negative words, and negative statements such as 'I will stop smoking,' are understood by the brain as, 'I want to smoke'. For each goal, identify three strategies for achieving it. The language of the goal statement is important and a small tweak in wording can have an impact on attaining your goals. Many people say, "I have to….," but if "I have to" is replaced with "I get to…" the brain perceives an opportunity to learn and experience and new pathways will be created in your brain to incorporate the new experience. *This is the pathway to creating new habits.*

Creating new routines and structures can make it easier to establish a new habit. Create a structure and support system for self-awareness by making time for reflection three times a day, reflective conversations with your buddy coach, or through any good routines that help you. The process of reflection is continual and will continue to feature in the following chapters.

For more knowledge and understanding:
- Search the net with relevant keywords, such as self-leadership, self-awareness, and reflective conversations.

- Meditation apps to awaken your mind and discover your values.
- Practice self-awareness for self-leadership, or follow a self-leadership guide.
- Practice body, mind, and spiritual awareness through the work of Deepak Chopra.

So far on your journey of awareness, have you felt like you are multitasking and doing too much too fast? You may ask, isn't multitasking a good thing to do? Research has shown that when we multitask, we often end up with lower productivity as we have no reserves of attention and can't act with self-awareness. So, to be more productive you may need to slow down. Does that sound wrong? Read on.

RELEASE THE HOSTAGE

Exercise: draw up some web diagrams to develop your self-awareness.

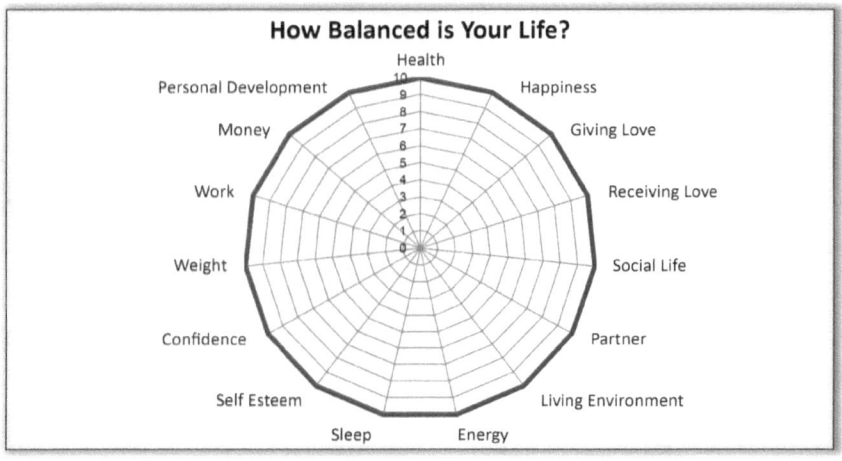

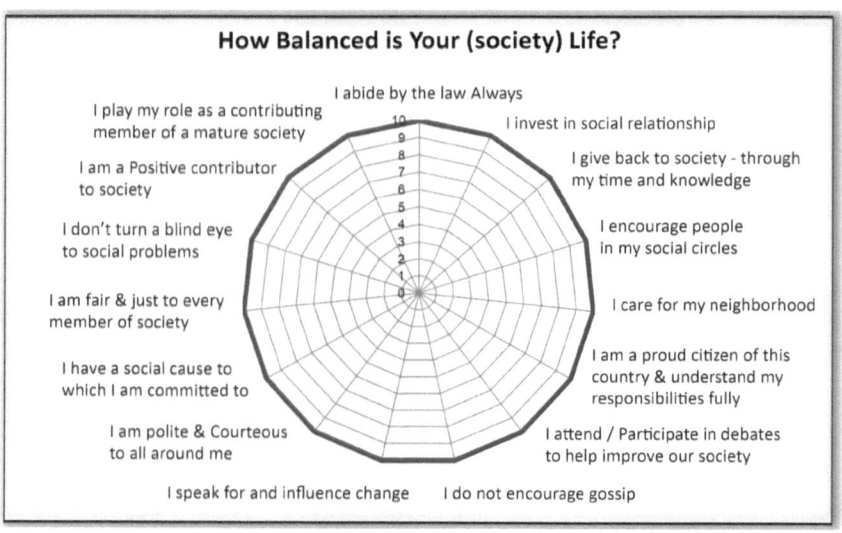

CREATE AWARENESS, IT IS THE FOUNDATION

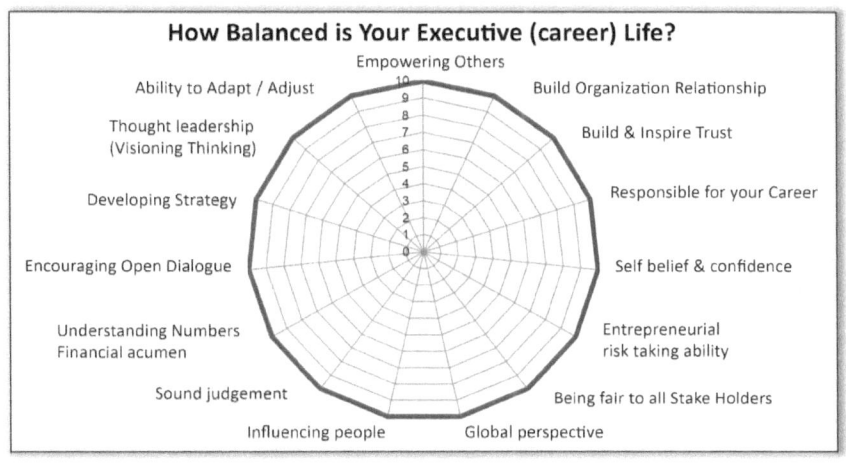

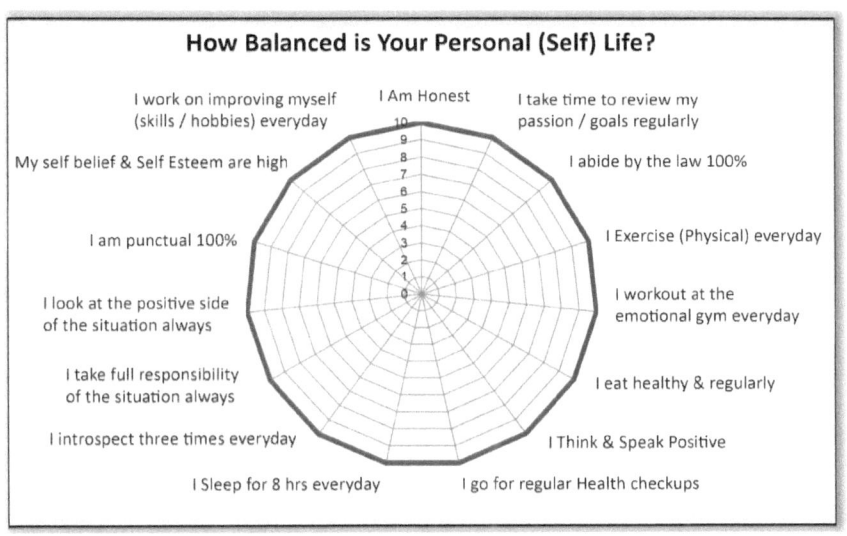

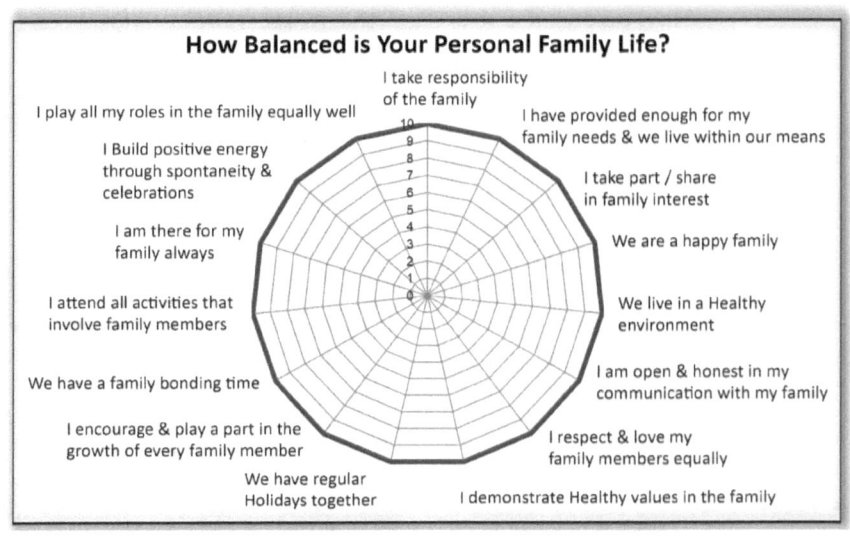

5

SLOW DOWN IF YOU WANT TO GO FAST

*"We are what we repeatedly do.
Excellence, then, is not an act, but a habit."*

— ARISTOTLE

In the movie *The Secret*, Michael Beckwith described the infinite life force:

> *"Regardless of what has happened to you in your life, regardless of how young or how old you think you might be, the moment you begin to think properly, there's something that is within you, there's a power within you that's greater than the world. It will begin to emerge. It will take over your life. It will feed you. It will clothe you. It will guide you, protect you, direct you, sustain your very existence…if you let it."*

This inner peace and power that every one of us has are about acknowledging, appreciating, accepting, and allowing the events in our lives to emerge. This requires a sort of quiet courage which only some of us demonstrate but we are all capable of. This inner power is a sort of a guidance system within us and, if we can tap into it, this system becomes the gateway to reaching our highest potential. This guidance system can shape our beliefs and values and at its core lies the answers to the questions which may have yet remained unanswered. The real you (*who am I?*) is at the core and is awaiting the day when you will be ready to accept it.

Slowing down is about creating a space for you to access this guidance system. This chapter will help you tap into the guidance system through three concepts: *the speed of presence, PQ brain, and meditation*. It may sound easy, but you will only move toward self-awareness if you make it a habit to tap into this system.

In his book, *Daily Rituals: How Artists Work*, Mason Currey wrote about the habits, routines, and rituals of artists including Benjamin Franklin, Karl Marx, and Ernest Hemingway. Benjamin Franklin kept it simple. He believed in blocking periods of time out for learning, mundane work, and deep work when he was not to be disturbed. He also made a habit of going to bed at the same time each evening, and getting up at the same times each morning. Karl Marx loved to spend the day in the library, reading and working through the night, while Earnest Hemmingway preferred to write in the early morning with the rising light and stop only when he knew what would happen next. Even though their rituals varied wildly, each one followed a routine that put them in the optimal state of mind for creativity. Sachin Tendulkar also had a set of rituals that he performed before going in to bat. For a few years, I had the good fortune to be a neighbour of Pandit Hariprasad Chourasia, a maestro, a classical flautist. I would wake up every morning to the divine sound of his playing the flute. He told me, "If I don't practise for a month my audience will know, if I don't practise for a week my critics will know, if I don't practise for a day I know."

Rituals are about setting up the day ahead. We get up and rush mindlessly to get ready to rush to work and the whole day pans out at a similar pace. If you can't sip your coffee while you smell it you are missing out on productivity. Morning and evening routines will set you up for success. They help you achieve more than you planned, think deeper, and do work that matters. They keep you at a steady pace throughout your day and make sure you do the most important things. This chapter is all about being more productive.

Have you thought about the first hour after you wake up, the first hour at the office, and how they impact your day?

Sip your coffee while you smell it

Everyone has experienced the calming effect of visiting a beach, or a forest or a mountain top, or a marvel of nature like the Jog Falls or the Niagara Falls. You will have experienced both the fury of nature and its calm beauty. Our response to this experience is a feeling from within. Time moves slowly and allows us to enjoy the beauty, which feels endless. We are at ease and have a feeling of inner peace which we do not want to end. You will have noticed that everything slows down before it speeds up again.

This inner feeling of calm and peace is also experienced when our productivity is at its height and has been beautifully described by Trace Hobson as the *Speed of Presence*. To really know something, you need to experience it, and this is true for the speed of presence. When you are at the speed of presence, you somehow know instinctively what the next steps are. There is a feeling of joy and a sense of satisfaction. It is as though the parts and the whole of you come together to give a sense of security that all is well. Being present in this way will give you access to more information and you will know what to do even when you don't know what to do. The speed of presence allows you to take care of everything, especially yourself, and you will gain a strong feeling of your authentic self or being.

When you are aligned and fully present with the person, place, or thing you are with, you are at the speed of presence. When you are with someone, there is a space between you and the person. Similarly, when you are in a place, there is a space between you and the place where you are. It is in these spaces that thoughts, feelings and emotions enter as disturbances and don't allow you to be fully present. If you can treat this space as sacred and not allow anything to come between you and the other person or the place, you will be fully present. When you reflect or meditate you will realise that there is a space between you and yourself that is sacred and which you can keep free from all disturbances. When disturbances are kept out, this sacred space will give you feedback in a continuous loop of self-awareness.

So, why do we find it difficult to stay at the speed of presence?

It is because we feel uncomfortable with ease, calm, and peace. Thoughts of missing out often come to us in this state and we feel restless and want change. In this VUCA[3] world of moving pieces, we find it difficult to be an observer and want to be engaged and involved. We add ourselves to the moving pieces and become a part of the volatile and complex puzzle.

Our social culture and education system are the environment we live in and this environment compels us to compete and aim to be the best. To understand what "best" is, we compare ourselves with others which makes us even more competitive and insecure. Our biggest saboteur, *"the judge"* in us, pushes us to try and constantly do better. And when you question this need to be the best, the judge will turn your attention onto others' weakness and makes you feel happy that you are better than them. This is the judge's way of protecting you from the challenge of self-awareness. More about the judge and our other saboteurs later.

The way to stay at the speed of presence is to stay anchored and aligned, to use a golfing term. Many golf players are told to slow down their swing to keep their body movements aligned and are then able to get their body weight behind the ball. What the golfer does is stay down a bit longer than usual and focus on the ball until the point of contact. Then they hit the sweet spot and their belief in the club begins to rise. They enjoy the rhythm.

Is there a rhythm to life?

In your journey to awareness, begin to be aware of the speed at which you talk, the speed at which your mind moves, the speed at which

---

[3] Volatility, Uncertainty, Complexity, and Ambiguity

you eat, and how patient you are with people and events. Are you comfortable with the rhythm?

When we compete and fear losing, we move faster than is comfortable. We are part of natures' energy cycle and need to be at a certain frequency to be in harmony with the cycle. If we are too fast, the law of diminishing returns kicks in and we become less productive. With fear comes anxiety, stress, tension, and resistance. Along with fear comes energy that often helps us to finish the job at the eleventh hour. But while this energy helps us manage deadlines, it often makes us reactive when we interact with others.

When you slow down, you begin to interact and listen with intent. Listening with your mind, heart, and soul brings out the best in you. You become better at interpreting and translating what you hear meaningfully. When you listen with intent, you will also experience a surge in energy that propels you forward and will help you to respond well in interactions, instead of being reactive. So, listening helps and benefits two people. When you listen with intent, you can't imagine the impact you have on the speaker. Being heard allows the speaker to take responsibility for what they are saying. Avi Kluger's research has shown that good listeners create good speakers, and good listeners are also good performers. A salesperson who listens well to the customer sells more. A physician who listens well to the patient diagnoses better, and so on.

> *Listen to every signal and every alert that tells you to slow down. If you ever feel your productivity is below your best, ask if you are missing a signal that the system has thrown at you.*

Recently, I experienced "Unhurried Conversations" facilitated by Farah Ismail, a fellow coach at our Bangalore Chapter. I urge you to try this activity with your team members. It's very simple. Any person in the group of eight to ten people who wants to speak has to pick up an item close to them – it could be a pen, a marker, anything at all – and hold it up for others to see. As long as this person wants to speak and continues to speak, they hold up the prop. Another person shall speak only when this person has put down the prop. This is an amazing experience and I urge you to try it. At the end, share your experiences with the rest of the group.

Strengths can sabotage you

> "If you don't like something, change it;
> if you can't change it, then change
> the way you think about it."
>
> — Mary Engelbreit

First, you need to know what to change. After reading the last chapter about self-awareness, you may now be aware of habits that you want to change. Your habits are ingrained patterns of behaviour that have become automatic and involuntary. When you enter a situation, your senses scan the information available and if your brain finds similar past experiences that can guide your responses in the present, you may not be prompted to consciously make decisions about how to act. The brain does this efficiently and automatically to save us from the cognitive effort that is needed to engage the prefrontal parts of the brain that consciously think and make decisions. Habits get stronger over time if they are not consciously challenged, even if they lead to poor outcomes. So, to change habits we need to make a conscious effort to decide how to behave, instead of relying on habit. This kind of conscious effort creates new pathways in the brain that we can then use when we are next in a similar situation, instead of the old habit. The brain has this remarkable adaptive ability of neuroplasticity to rewire itself in response to new experiences and our conscious efforts. While we can't erase the mental pathways of our old habits, they will fade over time if we consciously create and use new pathways.

I love the way Shirzad Chamine presented the PQ brain in his book. Imagine three different regions in the brain. In one region, your *saboteurs* reside and act as headwinds as you try to achieve your goals. Saboteurs include the *judge*, the *controller*, the *avoider*, the *victim*, and the *stickler*. In a second region lives your *sage*, who handles challenges positively with curiosity, empathy, creativity, calm, and clear-headed laser-focused action. Your *sage* helps you perform at your peak and experience joy and satisfaction.

Saboteurs are responsible for the behaviours we want to change. Frequently, we don't realise when a strength has become a saboteur. Let's say you have an eye for detail, which is usually a good attribute to have as long as it's turned on the right targets. But the moment you cast your eye for detail over other people's work, you risk interfering and micro-managing. With a strong need to win, you risk pushing to win at all costs and becoming a leader who tramples on others and is resented. The actions of our various saboteurs hold us hostage. Our limiting beliefs arise from our saboteurs and operate through them.

Just as when you touch a hot stove you automatically pull your hand away, Chamine tells us that negative emotion should prompt you to instantly move away from the saboteur to the sage. By reacting immediately, you will create muscle memory. This is what lies in the third region of the brain: the *self-control muscle*. We need to strengthen the self-control muscle by staying in the moment and consciously responding to people and events. This is the essence of working at the speed of presence, in the now.

Be in the now

Being in the present, in the now, you experience freedom. Freedom is experienced when you surrender to what has stopped you from moving ahead. Leave the fight and drop it like a hot potato. The impact of holding on to negative thoughts can be devastating.

Here, again, learning to stay in the now is the development of a new skill and you must practise this skill to mastery. How can we move from unconscious incompetency to unconscious competence? Through the *power of silence*. Silence is a very effective tool in my coaching sessions and the way to find silence is through meditation.

Close your eyes and focus on your thoughts. Observe the thoughts that come and go. Let them come and go naturally. Don't evaluate or judge or dive into the thoughts. As one thought passes by gently, say "*next*" and await the next thought. The word *next* becomes an anchor to keep you from following the tide of your thoughts. Slowly, you will find that your thoughts dissolve and you begin to feel the silence. In that moment, everything stops and time feels frozen. Continue to experience the silence by being a detached witness.

Spiritual partnering practice

Another approach to meditation is to anchor yourself to your breath. Begin by exhaling slowly through the mouth until you feel your lungs are empty and then take a slow deep breath in through the nose. Repeat three or four times and allow yourself to settle into a comfortable breathing pattern. Focus on your breath and use a small piece of your awareness to say, "Breathe". With every breath, say, "breathe," but if you hear, say, a dog barking, identify what you hear or feel by saying it, "dog barking." Then bring yourself back to anchor your breath. Continue for ten to twelve minutes.

Deep breathing is a meditation practice. First, exhale completely and then take a long, slow, deep breath. A variation is to break your deep breath down into six smaller continuous inhalations: Breathe one, stop (hold), breathe two, stop (hold), breathe three, stop (hold), and so on to the sixth breath. By the time you have inhaled for the sixth time, you will feel the oxygen from your throat to deep down in your lungs. Then exhale slowly in six smaller exhalations until your lungs are empty. Repeat the breathing pattern at your comfort level and practise in the morning and two to three times daily.

Take a morning walk every day and stop along the way to focus on a leaf or flower. Feel the different textures and identify the different shades and colours. When walking, focus on an object from a distance and stay focused until you come close. Do you see anything different?

Place your fingertips at the top of your forehead and very slowly run them down along the contours of your face. Focus on the physical sensation in your fingertips.

Place your right hand on your heart and feel the heartbeats through your fingertips.

Place your right hand on your stomach and feel the rise and fall of your stomach with every breath.

Rub two fingertips together very gently to feel the ridges on your fingertips. Rub the fingertips of one hand gently against the fingertips and palm of the other hand. Focus on the sensations.

Sit quietly with your eyes closed and listen to all the sounds in your environment. Try to identify the sounds. Listen to the sound furthest away from you, then listen to the sound closest to you. Try to hear your breathing.

At the office in a meeting, you could feel the edge of the table, feel the texture, feel the temperature of the cup of tea that you are drinking or the glass of water that you have picked up. Rub two fingers gently. Focus on the sensations.

Taste and feel the texture of the food you are eating.

You need to focus on your senses to be present. The moment of focus is the same as the focus needed for presence. Practising focus trains the self-control muscle to help you switch off the saboteurs and turn to the sage when you feel triggers for negative beliefs. To be at the speed of presence you need to practise focus every day.

Using these practices, you can create a routine of positive habits that will set the stage for your transformation to a higher level of leadership and productivity.

My morning routine

The first thing I do when I wake up each morning is express my gratitude for another energising day ahead. I look for reasons to smile and feel happy. I wake up early so I don't need to jump out of bed. I sit on the edge of the bed for a few minutes before I start my day. In these few moments, I think of the day ahead and what is important for me to be aware of. I keep the smile going.

After I freshen up I begin my observations in meditation. I could be engaged with any of the meditation practices I have described in different combinations for up to twenty minutes.

Then I go for my morning walk for an hour. My observations continue. I use this time to remind myself that I want to be at the speed of presence. For the first forty minutes, I walk briskly, followed by ten minutes of stretches. For the final ten minutes, I walk at a leisurely pace. Throughout my walk I keep the smile going.

Throughout the meditation and walk, I listen to soft classical music and smile a lot and this is therapeutic.

I spend the next twenty minutes reading the newspaper and sipping my tea with breakfast.

I have a strict rule that there are no phone calls or any other disturbances during this sacred time every morning. This is *My Time*

I encourage you to set a routine that you believe in completely. Slow down if you wish to go fast and the rest of the day you will be surprised how productive you are. It is important to keep your hobbies going as part of your routine. For me, it has always been sport. First, it was cricket and badminton. Later, it was squash. And now, it is golf, twice a week.

Go ahead and make your routine. To reap the benefits, it must be authentic and you must believe in it.

Some suggested reading and online search terms:

Speed of presence, Trace Hobson.
positiveintelligence.com – Shirzad Chamine. Do take the test he offers, to know your saboteurs.
avi-kluger.com
Energising your chakras Coacharya – Ram Ramanathan
Unhurried conversations

Throughout your routine, you are by yourself and have been communicating with yourself. You have been reflecting, evaluating, planning, and executing, in your mind. How you communicate with yourself is critical. Most of us understand communication as interacting with others, but both internal and external communication are critical to your success. Communication is simple, but not well understood. In the next chapter, we will explore communication and you might be surprised at how much language can shape your perspective.

6

COMMUNICATIONS CONNECT PEOPLE

"The most important thing in communication is to hear what isn't being said."

— PETER DRUCKER

Converse to be happy

Communication will work for you only if you work at it. Sharpen your communication skills to ensure your meaning is understood and you understand others' intent. How often do we reflect on the meaning of our communication before we speak? How often do we listen to reply rather than to understand? One of the problems of corporate communication is that we think speaking is communicating. We believe that, since we have spoken our thoughts, we will be understood exactly the way we intended. But, when was the last time you checked whether your message had been understood?

Communication may be the most stimulating part of leadership, but it also the most difficult. I took a course on communication in my B school. Even there, the syllabus didn't consider how the listener was perceiving what we said. But the characteristics of the listener should be central when we plan communication. The essence of communication should be to ensure that our meaning is clearly understood. The magic of effective communication lies in the space between meaning and perception.

In my decades in the corporate world, I realised that as I rose in the hierarchy, people began to take even my mere suggestions seriously. It was as though that was the way things were done. But I was thinking aloud, without being aware of what I was communicating. Now, thinking aloud is not a crime, but we need to think through the way our communications are understood before we speak, especially as we gain more power and authority.

> "To effectively communicate, we must realise that we are all different in the way we perceive the world and use this understanding as a guide to our communication with others."
>
> — Anthony Robbins

The impact of communication is the residual feeling

When we attend an important meeting, we start communicating even before we speak. As our anxiety or excitement take over, our systems react and cortisol or oxytocin are released. This chemical release makes our hearts beat faster and activates neural networks. The network activated depends on our relationship with the person we are meeting and could be either the *protect/fear* network or the *trust* network.

How does this impact your communication?

If the person you are meeting has similar anxieties or emotions, how will your communication be received?

In most communication, the message received will not be identical to what the speaker intended. The receiver's interpretation of the message will be influenced by a variety of factors, including their feelings and the importance of the meeting to them. Their interpretation will also depend on their history of similar interactions and what people retain from past interactions. Interpretation is also more than the words that were said. How we think, feel, and act, are all implicated in how we communicate and our influence on others. Unfortunately, our education systems focus on language and neglect the behavioural and emotional elements of communication for both speakers and listeners.

Communicate to understand

In her book *Conversational Intelligence,* Judith E. Glaser explained how to move beyond fear to build trust through more meaningful dialogues. Glaser classifies conversations into three levels, from routine to discovery.

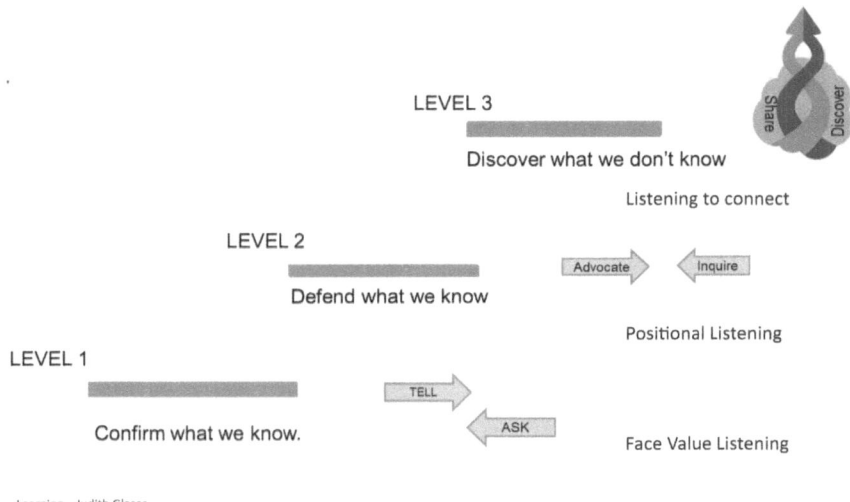

Learning – Judith Glaser

Level 1 – face value listening. At this level, we converse in the drama stage and speak for dramatic effect from an entrenched point of view. Our conversational intent is not to understand the other and be understood, but to confirm what we know and we are attached to being right. Speakers who genuinely have the other person's interest at heart don't converse at this level. Listening at this level is also at face value, without attention to the speaker's meaning.

Level 2 – positional listening. This stage is transitional between speaking for dramatic effect and the situation stage in the engagement patterns model. At this level, when a group is trying to work strategically towards *what next*, you will defend what you know and what you believe is the only correct perspective. In this stage, people look for distortions and deletions from what they hear. They tend to take a fixed perspective when listening and focus on what they think is the way forward, rather than listening to others' perspectives.

Level 3 – listening to connect. The third level of conversation shifts to childlike curiosity and discovery. Communication at this level is about sharing and being curious to know and understand more, to discover what we don't know. Conversing is based on the assumption that you don't know enough or you don't know everything.

Most of us believe that we have done our homework and know what we need to know. But if you start communicating with the assumption that you don't yet know enough, you may be surprised at how the conversation goes. At level 3, conversing is like peeling an onion, layer after layer, to get to the core. You begin to connect with the other person at a deeper level. Our brains are wired for connection and listening, and conversing at level 3 allows us to develop the trust that is needed for healthy conversations and relationships to flourish.

Generative listening helps expand the self

I recently heard Ram Ramanathan speak of another level of communication. While level 3 involves listening for discovery and understanding, Ramanathan's next level involves *generative listening*, which he explained through a story from the *Mahabharata*. Arjuna was confused on the battlefield and had more questions than answers. Lord Krishna decided to show his real power and expanded to show Arjuna his true self. Now, Arjuna was considered another form of the Lord himself, so Krishna was demonstrating to Arjuna the potential he himself had to grow. Generative listening is also dynamic co-creation. When we open our minds to silence and let go of thoughts, emotions, and feelings as they come along, listening becomes much more than hearing the words that are said. At the level of generative listening, we also attend to what is not said and so connect with future potential.

While these models of conversation focus on in-person interactions, their insights could also apply to the leadership relationship. Leadership is convincing people to align with a vision and feel its energy. To do so, leadership must create trust so that people feel confident to pursue the shared potential or goal, rather than maintain status quo.

Glaser outlined 5 "Conversational blind spots":

Blind spot 1 – We assume that the other person is like us, sees what we see, thinks what we think, and feels what we feel. We forget that they see the world through a different lens. They have their own patterns of interpretation and absorption that are different from ours.

Blind spot 2 – Others' experiences have shaped their values and beliefs and they see the world differently. We assume others see an issue the way we see it. We fail to recognise that fear and mistrust change the way we see and interpret reality.

Blind spot 3 – We find it difficult to empathise with others as the experiences that have shaped us are different. To empathise, we must listen with an open mind and heart and with childlike curiosity. Empathy requires honesty and transparency. We need to operate at the speed of presence.

Blind spot 4 – We think that we retain or remember from our previous interactions what the other person said. Instead, we retain what we understood and not what we did not hear or understand. What we understood may be distorted due to biases developed through experience.

Blind spot 5 – A major assumption made by many of us is that the meaning of the message lies with the speaker. We are often unaware that there are different ways to interpret the message. When we say something and have our meaning in mind, we tend to believe that the listener shares the same thought processes and has received our meaning directly. Rather, meaning is created within the listener's understanding.

Conversations with ourselves are as stimulating as coffee

So far, we have seen that we need to change the way we converse with others. But, have you given serious thought to how you communicate with yourself? How often do you communicate with yourself? Are you conscious of every occasion that you tell yourself something? Much of the time, our cognitive processes are unconscious and automatic and we are not aware of our decision-making. For example, when you choose task A over task B, you may attribute your decision to a reasoned choice, but the process unfolds without conscious deliberation if the response has been remembered and become habitual. When these unconscious habits are understood as reasoned choices, they can become limiting beliefs that strengthen the habit. To move away from limiting beliefs and habits, we need to make our choices conscious again.

Every conversation we have, externally or internally, has an impact on our IQ, EQ, and SQ. *Spiritual Quotient* (SQ) is the Quotient of *presence in the moment*.

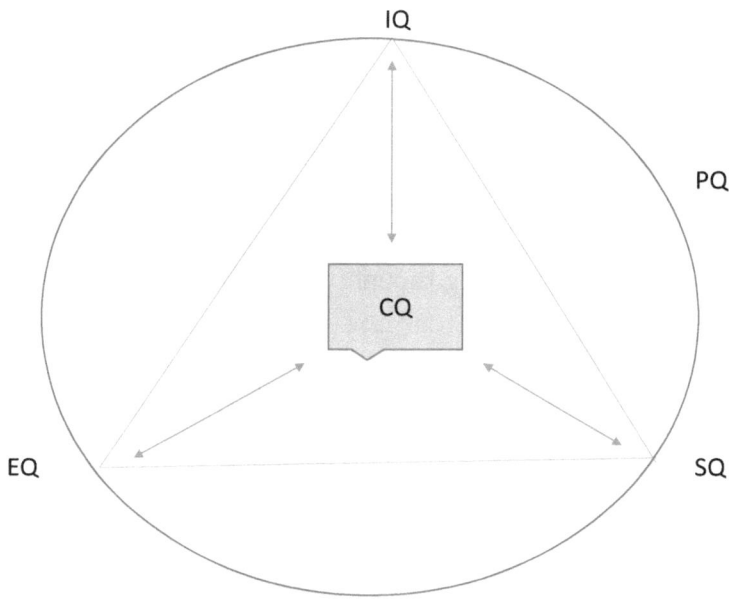

CQ = Communication Quotient, EQ = Emotional Quotient, SQ = Spiritual Quoient, IQ = Intelligence Quotient, PQ = Positive Quotient

You may have heard about Ek Lavya. When he was rejected by Dronacharya and not accepted as his pupil, he made a clay statue of Dronacharya, his guru, and learned the art of archery. We all know that a clay statue can't teach you archery. Ek Lavya would hide behind bushes and listen to the conversations between Dronacharya and Arjuna. Ek Lavya developed insights and learning from listening to these conversations. What helped him to master their teachings was his continuous practice of listening for discovery and understanding by being present in the moment. For him to develop deep understanding and the insights needed to master archery, he needed to listen keenly with his mind, heart, and soul. Ek Lavya must have been at the speed of presence to master the art of listening. Or, did his listening skills help him to be at the speed of presence?

Do you listen to yourself?

Many times in a day you might say, "I don't like this" or "I wish I could have more influence on my team" or "Oh, I am so stressed out" and so on. These conversations with yourself are often at an unconscious level. If you heard the same statements from someone else, what would you think?

Take the example of a negative self-communication, "I don't like math", or, "I don't understand technology." What is this self-talk doing to your IQ? When you tell yourself that you don't like or understand something, your brain accepts that this is true and shuts off attention to the avenues that could help you to understand more. By closing off the learning process, negative self-talk stops you from using your intellectual capacity to its full potential. Limiting beliefs develop and prevent you from choosing to learn more.

Take another example. You've had a tough meeting and the judge in you begins to tell you that the person you met with was unreasonable. You refuse to see their point of view and start believing that they were unreasonable. The belief does not start strong but gathers momentum with every subsequent meeting when you don't consciously reconsider whether it was true. Soon enough, you have labelled the person as unreasonable without ever fully understanding their point of view. Imagine what this self-talk has done to your EQ. Will it hurt your relationships with your team? Yes, if you attend to similar behaviour patterns and label them unreasonable, then you will also start labelling others as unreasonable.

Think about how you address monotonous work. Do you look forward to it, or do you dismiss it as boring? Do you tackle mundane work with energy, or do you resign yourself to it? What effect does this approach have on your presence in the moment? Are you at the speed of presence? What about when you meet someone for the first time? Are you apprehensive and anxious, or do you see an opportunity to meet someone interesting from whom you might learn something new? What impact is your attitude having on your SQ?

Our communication with ourselves has a deep impact on our IQ, EQ, and SQ. These effects limit our ability to listen with the intention to be present. If we are not at the speed of presence then our productivity is lowered. The impact of negative self-communication on our IQ, EQ, SQ lowers the balance of positive energy- PQ – in our system that we need for deep relationships.

Do we listen to our customers with intent to understand their concerns, do we empathise with them? Let me share an experience of mine. At Airtel, our Customer Care division was run efficiently and was critical to our success. In 2002, the call centre had a surge of calls from customers in Mysore who complained that they could not make calls. This was interpreted to be due to congestion in the network. The tests conducted by the technical department showed congestion of only 8% in two towers during the peak hours. Customers continued complaining, and we could not identify what was causing the problem. When the problem was not solved, the customer care department, the technical department, and the leadership team decided to have our next customer meeting in Mysore.

On the way to the meeting, we discussed the complaints we had received from the region. A group of customers were threatening legal action and we were expecting a tough time with some customers at the meeting, but we were looking for solutions and wanted to find a *win/win* solution. Usually, we would expect around four hundred customers at a customer meeting, but over fifteen hundred customers attended this one. Not all of them were Airtel customers, but the crowd didn't want us to verify whether everyone was an authentic customer, and there wasn't enough time if we were to start our meeting on time. So, we let the crowd in and started the meeting.

It began peacefully enough, but suddenly a group of customers started shouting. First, they threw papers in the air and then chairs and tables were thrown. Before we realised what was happening, my Vice President of Sales, Shankar, and I were in the middle of a shouting crowd. The situation was getting out of control and the Police Inspector, whose squad had been asked to attend the meeting as a precaution, joined the crowd and climbed onto a table to tell us we should listen to the customers as they paid our salaries. My first thought was to tell him that taxpayers like us were the ones who paid his salary. But then, I realised that what he said made sense. The customer pays our salary.

After two more tense hours, I told the Police Inspector to disperse the crowd or I would be forced to complain to the Commissioner of Police at Bangalore. Asking Shankar to follow me and, being kicked and punched by the crowd, we forced our way out without protection.

While this commotion was going on, our managers managed to speak to some customers to get a more detailed understanding of the issue. Mysore was expanding rapidly, with IT giants setting up offices. People who came to work in central Mysore bought telephone connections in the heart of the city but lived on the outskirts. Phone coverage was not an issue while they were at work, but when they went home they were cut off. In hindsight, the issue was simple, but it was blown out of proportion because we did not listen to the customers. They were complaining of coverage and we heard it as call drops. If we had only listened with our mind, heart, and soul, this misunderstanding and all the trouble could have been avoided. It was an expensive mistake, but in hindsight, it was a small price to pay for a BIG lesson learned – always listen to your customers with intent.

Make intelligent communication a practice

Every conversation you have is an opportunity to experience conversing at level 3. Start with open-ended questions and use the conversation to dive deep and explore what you don't know. By being aware of your blind spots, you can consciously test your understanding and experience greater insight.

Now you need to test the insights and learning that you have gained so far to experience deep learning. This begins the process of creating new pathways in the brain to change limiting beliefs and negative habits. While reading gives you knowledge and understanding, only when you take it to the emotional or the heart level will deep transformation begin. Some of you may be wondering, "How do I begin?" Start by writing down a few statements you could use to open a conversation at level 3. What deep dive statements or questions could you frame? Write them down. Just like practising cricket skills in the net, you need to practise the skills of listening for understanding. Start with the example questions below and add your own questions.

Questions to help open a level 3 conversation:

- What assumptions do you hold about this project?
- If these assumptions are true, what would the outcome be?
- Help us understand this better.
- Who should we keep informed?
- What issues are top of mind for you? What are your insights here?
- How do you think our customers see this?
- Would you like to share your experience with this situation, so far?
- If we had the resources, what would your plan be?
- Would you please share your idea with us?
- What do you want to achieve with this idea?
- What is your vision of success? What is our desired outcome?

Questions to dive deep and understand more:

- What should I do to make level 3 communication a habit?
- How do I remain consciously aware of my blind spots?
- How does the speed of presence affect my listening skills?
- What is empathy? What do I need to do to empathise with the other person?

Some more resources to help you to a deeper understanding:

- Judith Glaser, *Intelligent Conversations*.
- Search the internet for videos of Judith Glaser talking about her research on conversations.
- Worksheets – what do I need to stop telling myself?
- Write down your blind spots (which experiences support the blind spots and how do you want to change what you do?)
- Write down statements to open a level 3 conversation and question to help dive deep.

Precise communication is critical for you to *release the hostage*. Pay special attention to how you communicate with yourself. You need to understand how the person you are communicating with interprets your statements. We need to understand how our brains interpret and respond to our conversations. We need to understand our cognitive processes so that we can use methods that will help us to make positive changes. For this, you need to carry your *SCARF* around. If you don't usually wear a SCARF, now is the time to start. The SCARF method will help you to re-program your brain to develop positive habits. Read on to design your own SCARF.

7

STRUCTURE TRUMPS CHAOS

"Mindfulness is a habit, it's something the more one does, the more likely one is to be in that mode with less and less effort…it's a skill that can be learned. It's accessing something we already have. Mindfulness isn't difficult. What's difficult is to remember to be mindful."

— David Rock

If you want to be in control of your destiny, you will change the way you speak to yourself. The word "can't" will disappear from your dictionary. You will look for meaning in everything you do and every move will be an opportunity to learn. Personally, I like to understand first at a cognitive level, and then experience what I have learnt at an emotional level through practise. Once I have experienced what I have learnt at an emotional level, my learning is deeper.

When it comes to rebooting our communication skills, we need to understand some neuroscience. I find it easiest to practice what I have learnt when there is a structure or model to follow and this is backed up by psychology and neuroscience. The brain finds it easier to learn and retain skills when we break them down into small, structured steps. To build a structure for practice, we need to identify the resources we need and then track our progress daily, weekly, and monthly. I have to thank the quality program, *Six Sigma*, for the important insight that *what is measured, can be improved upon*.[4]

> "We all often think about what's easy to think about, rather than what's right to think about."
>
> — David Rock,

In today's VUCA[5] world, it's important to understand what drives human behaviour. Human behaviour can be understood simply as the actions we take to minimise threats and maximise rewards. The same brain networks that are directed at minimising threats to our survival, drive us to create social networks to maximise rewards. This neural network produces two emotional states: *toward* or *reward*; and *away* or *threat*. When we are in a *towards* state, we are open to choices, opportunities, options and more available information to work with.

---

[4] The roots of Six Sigma as a measurement standard can be traced back to Carl Friedrich Gauss (1777-1855) who introduced the concept of the normal curve. Six sigma as a measurement standard was coined by Motorola.

[5] Volatile, Uncertain, Complex and Ambiguous

In the *towards* state, we experience the positive emotions of happiness, joy, engagement, and connectedness. On the other hand, the *away* state offers only limited choices and information and is associated with experiencing negative emotions of fear, frustration, and anger.

The brain's oldest systems operate for our survival and control our drives for food, water, temperature balance, and emotional responses. Conscious thinking and self-control of our behaviour, or executive function, takes place in a different, evolutionarily younger area of the brain, the prefrontal brain. Our emotions are based in the limbic brain and a tiny part of this is the amygdala. In the amygdala, the strongest *away* state is triggered in response to threats to our survival: the *fight or flight* response we have talked about. When we are not under threat, energy in the form of glucose is directed to the prefrontal brain. However, if a threat triggers an *away* state when the fight or flight mode is activated, energy is directed instead to the areas of the body that prepare for fight or flight: the legs and hands. This limits our capacity to think consciously. Similarly, when we are too cold or hot, or hungry, energy is diverted to modulate our temperature or drive us to find more energy, and our capacity for conscious thought is limited. If we are with others, the brain continues to respond in this way but the threats are threats to our social "survival", such as when our social standing or relationships are threatened.

At INSEAD at Fontainebleau, I took a course on *Thinking Right* that was about using different frames to help define an issue correctly and think more deeply. David Rock created an ideal frame or structure for understanding social networks, *SCARF*. SCARF helps us understand the impact of our communication at a deeper level. The SCARF model will help us to be at the speed of presence and experience *being*.

The SCARF model

Status – Your relative importance to others
Certainty – Your ability to predict. The brain loves certainty.
Autonomy – Choice and control.
Relatedness – How we get along with others, and our sense of belonging and safety.
Fairness – Our perceptions of a fair exchange.

Status. The brain is constantly monitoring people's relative importance or status in any social group. Status could be real, or a perception based on social stimuli. When we experience increased social status, we move into a *towards* state. Similarly, losing social status could put us in an *away* state. When we are criticised in front of others and feel embarrassed or humiliated at the loss of social status, cortisol is released as part of a *flight* response. In this *away* state, we feel less secure and feel the drive to protect ourselves by escaping from the situation or attacking the cause of lost status.

People attach relative status to themselves and the person they are conversing with. The social status we assign to people depends on their comparative education, wealth, standing in society, experience, knowledge, and other valued traits. Social status can affect mental processes and a perceived potential or actual lowering of social status, which in turn can generate a strong fight or flight response that might render the conversation ineffective.

Social status is raised by experiences such as giving an appreciated suggestion in a classroom or business meeting, or telling a joke that makes the speaker feel engaged. The opposite is experienced when a leader micro-manages employees and is overly directive, generating an *away* state for team members who perceive that the boss thinks they are not good enough.

A person's perceived status increases when they feel they are being treated on the same level as their employer. When a manager openly shares and expresses their vulnerabilities, they treat themselves on a par with their employee, creating equal social status in the eyes of the employee. Giving positive feedback in public and acknowledging staff are positive ways to raise employees' status. Another tool to raise others' status is to acknowledge, appreciate and clarify your understanding with them. Seeking permission before giving feedback is an especially powerful tool to raise the relative status of the person you are communicating with and discourage a fight or flight response.

Certainty. The brain works automatically to recognise patterns and make automatic decisions about responding to future events based on past events. This is not a conscious process and the brain can be biased toward automatic processes rather than conscious deliberation to save us cognitive effort. Conscious thought requires effort, but when the brain relies on past experience to respond automatically to new events, without us needing to consciously make decisions, less cognitive effort is required. The brain does this to protect us and save energy.

Like a computer, the brain accesses our past actions, beliefs, and patterns in response to new situations. The brain is a very effective pattern recognition machine. Based on patterns retained from the past, the brain produces a response that it calculates is likely to be appropriate for the current situation. For example, we have learned from experience that we might burn our hand if we touch a hot stove, so we automatically recoil from touching it.

The brain also prefers certainty when responding automatically and we feel uncomfortable when something is not certain. This discomfort is the brain's way of telling us that conscious thought might be needed. A researcher studied two groups of marathon runners who were to run a race. The first group was given all the details for the race before it started, such as the route and where water sheds would be located. The second group was told only to follow the markers. This second group of runners who were not told what to expect during the race finished slower than the first group, and some runners did not even complete the course. This study showed how even a small amount of uncertainty can create errors by drawing cognitive effort away from the goal.

As a leader when you share your plans for executing a task, do you give your team the certainty they are looking for? Strategies for addressing certainty include setting the meeting context or asking the other person what they would like to achieve during the meeting. Do you have an agenda for the meeting and do you stick to it? In uncertain situations, just acknowledging the uncertainty can help put the team in a *towards* state. By expressing vulnerability or acknowledging uncertainty, a leader can prevent the amygdala from hijacking the team. A simple way to reduce uncertainty going forward is to create a structure for the team's expectations, such as by announcing a date for the next review meeting. People like working with reliable co-workers because of the certainty they exude. By behaving reliably, we can set up certainty and boost productivity.

Autonomy. Autonomy is the experience of choice and control. Greater autonomy is rewarding, while reduced autonomy can be de-motivating. When facing a task we don't want to, telling ourselves, "I have to do this," we move into an *away* state. However, when we feel constrained in this way, we can choose to create a *towards* state by consciously looking for choices. Research has established a strong connection between choice and health. Elderly retired people living in supported care residences who were offered choice and control over the meals they ate or their entertainment options showed a significant improvement in health. The more we are in control of our choices, the healthier we are.

When leaders adopt a *commanding* style and are overly directive, giving people direct instructions to follow, their teams experience reduced control and autonomy. In comparison, a level 5 leader (as described in the book *Good to great*) who asks team members about alternative courses of action or provides opportunities for choice, will increase team members' control and autonomy. By simply asking team members their preferences, such as between two alternative tasks, leaders can build autonomy. A mother who is looking for help from her children might try this. Asking a child whether they would prefer to wash or dry the dishes would certainly create fewer arguments.

Micro-management kills autonomy by taking choice away from people at every level but making space for creativity and exploration helps build autonomy. For sensitive meetings, such as an annual budgeting meeting, asking your team their preferences for the meeting date and location will help to bring them into the meeting in a *towards* state. When we are in a towards state, more energy is directed to the prefrontal brain for conscious thought, making us receptive to learning and creating insights.

Relatedness. People form groups or tribes with others who have common attributes. Do you feel part of a group or out of it? The worst *away* feeling is loneliness and people look for friends and a sense of belonging in their teams. The need to belong can be seen very clearly in team sports. Team members come to believe in the bond that is created to help the team play well and succeed. A great example of this was an opening pair in international one-day cricket, Saurav Ganguly and Sachin Tendulkar. Their strength fed each other and their connection and mutual understanding were so deep that they could communicate with a look.

When we visit a new country, we feel like a stranger because this relatedness is missing. But we soon begin to relate to places and events we have read about or would like to explore and begin to feel part of the new environment. What experiences have you had when meeting someone for the first time? Did you look for some common ground, friends in common, to begin building a relationship?

In a social environment, we are usually triggered to seek a sense of connection or feel a sense of threat if we don't think we can connect. When we meet someone who has been critical of us, we might feel less related to them in a meeting, but if they have appreciated us in the past, we experience a *towards* response and dopamine and oxytocin are released that make us feel good. *We are designed for connections.*

Fairness. People have a strong sense of what is just and fair. Just as you cannot have one set of rules for your son and another for your daughter, you cannot treat people or departments differently in an organisation. Everyone has to follow the same rules. If one person is allowed to work from home, the choice should be given to all. Fairness is about walking the talk and when you have values that you want the organisation to work by, they need to be demonstrated by all. Unfair behaviour or exchanges generate a threat response that could affect behaviour and productivity.

In studies of fair exchange, when a cash reward is distributed equally to all group members, people moved into a *towards* state, but when one group member is given less than others, the exchange is not perceived to be fair. What people consider to be fair will depend on their past experience and the structure they have agreed to work in.

If you ask your team member to come in early to work as an important project needs attention, but when they come in, they find you are not in the office early and you leisurely walk in after you've hit the gym and had a nice breakfast, what state do you think your team member might be in? I guess Keki Pardiwala, my boss in Finance at P&G, was aware of this when he spent twelve nights in the office with the team when P&G took over RHL in India and we had to submit audited results on a short deadline. Threats to perceived fairness can be reduced by increasing transparency and communication. Getting more people engaged in the organisation's operations and strategies would help build a feeling of fairness.

The SCARF model provides a robust framework for building self-awareness in ourselves and others. When combined with Daniel Goleman's EQ, SCARF provides a framework for building successful teams. The five domains of status, certainty, autonomy, relatedness, and fairness, are not only important to the brain but critical for collaboration and building relationships. When we want to use our communication skills to influence others, keeping the five domains in mind to increase the *towards* state will help us communicate effectively.

As we each operate in different environments, we will remember SCARF best if we can connect it to our own experiences. Use the worksheets below to develop a deeper understanding of SCARF. Write down your thoughts for each question.

SCARF worksheets

Status
1. How can we reduce the threat of reduced status in our workplace?
2. How can we increase people's rewards from increased status? What are the benefits?
3. Pick three members of your team and write down what you would do to increase their status.

Certainty
1. List opportunities to create greater certainty in your workplace.
2. To create certainty, what do we need to be clear about?
3. What does certainty do to us and our brains?
4. How do we reduce the threat from uncertainty?
5. How do we increase the rewards from certainty? What are the benefits of certainty?

Autonomy
1. Would greater autonomy for people in your organisation be helpful? How?
2. Are you willing to offer greater autonomy to your team members? What is your action plan?
3. List opportunities in your organisation to increase engagement.
4. How do you personally view autonomy?
5. How do you reduce threats to autonomy?
6. How do you increase the rewards of autonomy? List the benefits.

Relatedness
1. How do we build trust in our teams? Create a list.
2. Is complete transparency good or bad for your company? Provide reasons.
3. How do we prepare ourselves to meet an important person for the first time? What is anxiety? Share an example.
4. How do we reduce the threat of a lack of relatedness?

Fairness
1. How do you ensure fairness in your organisation?
2. How do you reduce the threat of unfairness?
3. How do you increase the rewards of fairness?
4. Do you have systems in place in your organisation to ensure fairness?
5. How do you ensure consistency in your behaviour to demonstrate fairness?
6. Have you been fair in the past? If not, what do you intend to do about it?
7. Which SCARF domains are your strongest and which are your weakest? How do you plan to improve in the weakest domains?
8. What patterns of the SCARF domains do you see in leadership you admire?
9. Are the systems in your organisation designed with this model in mind? Would you want to change it? How and when?
10. Which of the SCARF domains has a long-term impact?
11. Is there a relationship between status, certainty, autonomy, relatedness, and fairness?
12. Which of the SCARF domains generate the strongest rewards or threats?

This chapter is important for putting what you have learned into practice. You will need to put in the effort to consciously think through the SCARF model and practice the five domains to be the master of your destiny. It's a good time to choose a buddy coach to work through the book with you, bring in a different perspective, and help create insights. If you don't have a buddy coach, create your own Excel spreadsheet for measurements and reflect on the data you record. For measurements, record the number of opportunities that were presented during the day and for how many of those you displayed the new behaviour, SCARF will help you demonstrate that you *care* about your people and *connect* with the people who matter to you. The model will bring into focus your appreciation for others and opportunities to build *trust*. When you connect and appreciate others, you will automatically relate more to the people who are with you on your journey. Being connected will take you away from conflict and allow you to engage at a deeper level where you can look for opportunities. More about the levels of engagement and building trust in the next chapter.

8

TRUST THIS GLUE

> "We need people in our lives with whom we can be as open as possible. To have real conversations with people may seem like such a simple, obvious suggestion, but it involves courage and risk."
>
> — Thomas Moore

Trust is the glue that binds our relationships. Trust is not built in one stroke, but through many small actions over time. One key ingredient for building trust is consistency. People look for consistent behaviour, and actions that match your words. Are you true to your word? Have you ever had your trust dented or broken?

There is little scientific literature about building trust. While many articles address the importance of building trust, the process itself is not fully understood. One reason for this is that trust is based on our behaviour patterns, and different situations call for different behaviour. So, trust looks different in different settings and is shaped by many variables. But across settings, trust is related to our character and personal behaviour. We are trusted because of our way of being and not by our appearance. Well-drafted communication may marginally help to build trust, but what and how you communicate is more important for building trust. How people understand and interpret your communication plays a big role in building trust.

Do you trust yourself before others trust you?

Trust yourself first

When you believe in your abilities and trust them, you learn to live to your potential. Self-trust is an important part of self-care as it allows you to have faith in yourself. Self-trust helps you get through challenging situations and teaches you to practise kindness to yourself. It even teaches us to forgive ourselves, which most of us find difficult. To build self-trust, learn to recognise your emotions and manage them positively. Build self-awareness of your thoughts and emotions and identify those that help and those that get in the way of building trust.

Self-trust requires you to be aware of your value system, ethics and standards. It pushes you in the direction that you want to pursue and will make you question yourself when you don't honour the commitments you have made to yourself. Self-trust will also make you reflect on the quality of time you spend with the people around you.

Every one of us has a judge inside. We might have needed this judge in our childhood days, but we don't need it in adulthood. However, the judge is a part of us and is difficult to get rid of. The judge pushes us to do better and protects us by making us believe we are better than others. How you communicate with yourself is how you communicate with the judge. When you agree with the judge, you are letting the judge dictate your judgements of people and label people. We need to engage our prefrontal brain and learn the art of consciously telling the judge, *"I have heard you, thank you"*, to come to more aware judgements.

We find it easier to forgive others than to forgive ourselves. Self-trust is also about showing compassion to yourself when you make a mistake. It is nurtured through connecting with your emotions and building the capacity to face your fears and face the unknown.

Self-trust takes you to self-leadership. One impact of self-leadership, when you observe and manage yourself, is the influence you have on your circle. With self-leadership, you take responsibility for your actions and behaviours. When you take responsibility, you may find the judge in you becomes active and tries to make you believe that criticising others will help you to move forward. When these limiting beliefs act up, learn the art of saying, "there goes my judge again." With self-leadership, you stop looking for approval and stop projecting authority onto others. On your journey to self-leadership, you will find yourself developing qualities of honesty, discipline, humility, love and compassion, accountability, courage, curiosity, assertiveness and self-belief.

Certainty is a trust pattern

I have heard people say, "I don't trust that person". Have you ever considered who starts the process of building trust? I have rarely heard a person say, "I will build trust with that person." The starting point for trust is for others to believe that you mean what you say. While I can't control whether others believe me, I can control what I say and what I commit to. Here, we are talking about the credibility which comes from being consistent. Commitment is based on two qualities: wisdom and integrity. Wisdom recommends, "Thou shall not commit to what you cannot deliver, and integrity commands, "Thou shall deliver what you have committed." Keeping your word shows others that you expect the same from them and they will be more likely to treat you with respect. In the process, further trust is developed. Consistently delivering on your commitments helps to build a pattern of trust. Team members look for consistency in our behaviour. Leaders who walk their talk earn high trust from their team. Leaders who are willing to co-create with team members show that they trust their team, and this builds further trust and helps to bring out the best in every team member. Be true to your word.

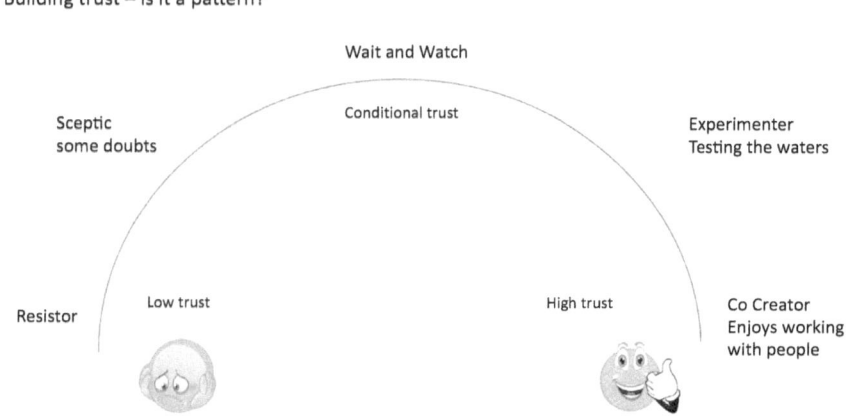

Building trust – is it a pattern?

Our system is designed for connections.
learning from Judith Glaser

The process starts with me

Truth-based trust is based on two aspects of our behaviour that can make us feel vulnerable: taking feedback and sharing our feelings. Are you ready to be vulnerable? Taking feedback from others, calls for courage. Taking feedback involves listening to other people's experience of your behaviour that you might not be aware of. Disclosing to others what you know about yourself that was not known to them will also build trust. If you are consistently vulnerable and open to feedback and self-disclosure, trust will be high and you will partner with others as co-creators.

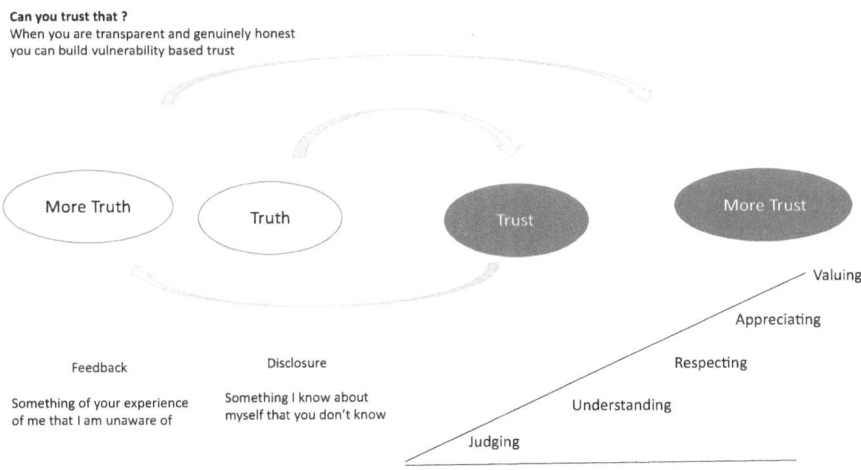

Do you trust yourself? If your answer is a strong *Yes* then it should be easy for you to understand the process of trusting others. Trusting yourself requires you to be completely honest with yourself. There is nothing to hide as your true self knows you completely. The same is true for building trust with others. Can you trust that?

Tool box to build trust

Bonding Experiences	Tolerance and Diversity	Truth and Trust
Shared Experience Shared Emotions e.g. White water rafting	Bonding requires differences which are non threatening	Trust is built on truth & sharing

From the book Care to Dare – George Kohlrieser

Bonding. Creating synergy through our attachment to others creates greater physical, emotional, intellectual, and spiritual energy than we can generate alone. Humans bond naturally – our brains are configured for connection. Bonding with others is a biological need and we develop our cognitive capacities throughout our lives by connecting and learning with others. Corporations often use team-building exercises such as white-water rafting, trekking, and rappelling, which require team members to rely on each other to help team members bond.

Tolerance and diversity. When we talk of diversity, we often mean gender or cultural diversity, but there are many more aspects to diversity. Being inclusive involves accepting the differences and diverse expectations of all employees. Each employee comes to work as a whole person and wants to feel wanted and included. How do we make sure each person is genuinely included as part of the whole? Inclusion calls for more than tolerance and patience and means adapting systems to work for everyone. Tolerance, patience, acceptance, and inclusion can only be practiced by being aware in the moment.

Truth and transparency. Being transparent and telling others about yourself calls for you to be courageous and willing to be vulnerable. Embracing vulnerability will make you a whole-hearted person. I first heard the concept of being whole-hearted from Dr Brene Brown. A whole-hearted person accepts vulnerability as part of everyday life and accepts all the emotions, including fear, anxiety, and sadness, along with joy, happiness, and fulfilment.

Happy employees make happy customers

Building relationships is all about trust. In the corporate world, we understand how employees who trust the organisation contribute more than those who are less engaged. Trust is the difference between the most productive employees and others. Trust is also an important part of engaging talent. Engaging candidates through their journey is one of the top competitive advantages a business can invest in. Trust and talent engagement is a formidable formula for success.

There are four levels of engagement, but we generally operate only in the first two – Drama and Situation. When I look back at the three decades I spent in the corporate world, I see that many meetings were not efficient as the outcomes could have been achieved in less than half the time. Most meetings began at the drama level of engagement, with people focused on who should the blame for errors be fixed on or why did we fail to foresee the challenges, and so on. Only after hours at the drama level would we say, "Ok, that happened, what should we do now?" and discuss the action we would take. The third level is when a participant has to exercise a choice about how they wish to engage. It was very rare to have a meeting and say, "let's explore the opportunities in front of us," which is the fourth level of engagement and truly the one to start with.

Engagement Patterns

Drama	How did we miss the signs/ lead indicators? Who is responsible? How much is the damage? Can you believe this is happening to our company?
Situation	How do we fix this issue? What is the solution to this issue? Will this new strategy work for us? What do we need, to get it right? How do make up the loss that it has left us with?
Choice	What are my choices? How do I relate to this issue? What is my choice?
Opportunity	What wants to happen? What are the opportunities here? What could be the emerging potential here?

Learning from Leon Vanderpol

In my five and half years at Airtel, I have a clear memory of one such meeting, and it turned our fortunes. In 2001, our Quality Compliance Manager, Mohan, came to me and explained the *price of non-conformance* (*PONC*) from Deming's theory of quality. At first, I found what he told me unbelievable. He said research had shown that the PONC in most companies is approximately 40% of the top line. After some deliberation, we decided to call a meeting of the leadership team to estimate the PONC of the Karnataka circle. Over two days, we listed the instances when we did not conform to the agreed targets or norms. Every event when we missed achieving the target was listed. We costed these events conservatively and yet, to our astonishment, still calculated that we were above the 40% mark. We decided to pick three of the targets we had not achieved and convert them into projects. We formed cross-divisional teams and created the Re1 project. The circle had agreed with the Board on a budget for an operating loss of around 300 million rupees. If we ran the projects well and engaged and motivated our people, we expected to close the year with a 1 Rupee operating profit. Instead, we closed the year with a profit of 180 million rupees. From then on, we were encouraged to think BIG.

If you value the softer aspects of building a corporate career, building trust is at the core and engaging with stakeholders is critical. If you don't practise these skills, your journey will be less fulfilling and your potential may be untapped.

Communicate well to engage and build trust

Good communication includes being clear about your commitments and what you have agreed on. Building trust is not without risk. It involves you and others taking risks on each other's trustworthiness. Effective communication is key to navigating the risk. Without effective communication, the messages you've intended to send may not be the messages that are received.

Practise effective communication by writing down the characteristics of the conversation types below to build your awareness and how you might use them. Explore how these conversations could help build trust and engagement with opportunity.

Co-creating conversations. How does co-creation create a culture that enables team members to create the future, invest in relationships, and co-create positive change?

Example: "What should we do to make it a reality?"

Aspiring conversations. How do you encourage your team members to think differently, think big? Is it about ideas? Is it through self-expression? Is it about what I believe in?

Example: "If we have the resources, what would you do to ensure a breakthrough?"

Expressing gratitude conversations. Are you able to say thank you from the heart, and do you mean it? Are you celebrating the small wins, are you expressing your gratitude to all stakeholders concerned?

Example: The year has come to an end and I must say, we as a team have performed brilliantly, thank you for your effort and commitment. I would like to acknowledge and express my gratitude to your families who have supported you all along."

Navigating conversations. To navigate, first seek to understand. Ask open-ended questions, and move the conversation towards a conclusion or a consensus.

Example: Help me understand that a bit more?"

Humanising conversations. Gallop studies and surveys have shown the value of appreciating people every day. If you can do that, humanising conversations will follow.

Example-"Thank you for delivering on time, I am sure our customer will appreciate this."

Clarifying conversations. Clarifying your understanding is the beginning of deep understanding. In questions try replacing why with what (Yes, you will rephrase your question) to experience the magic.

For example, "Why did you not meet your targets?" becomes, "What stopped you from achieving your targets?"

When you communicate to build trust by accepting feedback or sharing your blind spots, you will frequently feel vulnerable and exposed and you may not want to carry on. Trust me, trust the process, and trust that vulnerability can be a strength. Let's explore this together in the next chapter.

9

VULNERABILITY IS A STRENGTH

"Vulnerability is the only authentic state. Being vulnerable means being open, for wounding, but also for pleasure. Being open to the wounds of life means also being open to the bounty and beauty. Don't mask or deny your vulnerability: it is your greatest asset. Be vulnerable: quake and shake in your boots with it. The new goodness that is coming to you, in the form of people, situations, and things can only come to you when you are vulnerable, i.e., open."

— Stephen Russel

As a kid, I was so afraid. I was afraid of being left alone in a crowd, I was afraid of being left alone in this world. I was afraid of losing my little possessions, my toys, my cricket bat, my hockey stick. The way I looked at the environment and the world around me didn't help. I heard family, friends, and others talk about what was good for us and they agreed it was all about accumulating wealth and material comfort. In the pursuit of these goods dictated by my society, I began to be selfish. It was sad and hurtful enough to lose in sport. I was not ready to lose and be hurt in life.

Does the thought of being vulnerable make you afraid? I admit it scares me, but I hope to find courage again as I have in the past. Experience has taught me vulnerability is a risk worth taking. Trusting in the value of vulnerability helps me feel good about myself, and keeps my self-esteem high. It helps me feel good to hear my voice and be visible to people who matter. It helps take me closer to my true self. All of us have shied away from being vulnerable at times, and yet all of us have also accepted vulnerability at some time in our lives. We just need to make this our daily practice.

Face your fears

The fear of rejection makes us feel vulnerable. Remember your first date? What helped you overcome that fear of rejection? For me, it was the thought that the worst-case scenario was that she would say no, but that would not be the end of everything. When you reframe the scene, you can minimise the pain or fear and that little bit of courage would help us through.

We live in a VUCA world where volatility, uncertainty, complexity, and ambiguity create fear. Our biggest fear is often the fear of failure. What will the team think of me? Will I lose my job? How will it be reflected in my appraisal? Fear stops people from doing their creative and productive best. Our ideal image of ourselves is to be perceived as capable, smart, and valuable to the organisation. We want to be a go-to person who helps the organisation overcome challenges, but fear takes us away rather than towards happiness.

When we are fearful, we tend to move away from the problem and the people involved. We leave it to others to handle the issue or simply hope and pray that the problem disappears. When we wear the lens of fear, the fight or flight response can be triggered. We avoid the problem and may freeze.

Fear is an unproductive response to uncertainty, but it is one of the strongest motivations for most of us to stay in our comfort zone. When fear dominates, our primitive brain systems take over and our creative brain remains dormant. The gut network is activated and we act conservatively to avoid harm. By giving in to fear, our saboteurs drive us to develop patterns of self-protection. Over time, these patterns become automatic and defensive behaviour patterns.

As a leader, do your team members fear you or see you as a secure base? Are you comfortable with them making mistakes, and do you allow them to experience and learn? A vulnerable leader creates a psychologically safe environment for a team to trust each other and be willing to try new ideas and speak their minds.

Vulnerability is courage

How does Dr Brene Brown see vulnerability?

> *"I define vulnerability as emotional risk, exposure, uncertainty. It fuels our daily lives. And I've come to the belief — this is my 12th year doing this research — that vulnerability is our most accurate measurement of courage — to be vulnerable, is to let ourselves be seen, to be honest."*

Dr Brene Brown describes vulnerability as the birthplace of innovation, creativity, and change. To create is to make something that has not existed before. There's nothing more vulnerable than that. Being adaptable to change is all about vulnerability. To be vulnerable is to display courage. Courage is a Latin word that means telling your story from the heart. Courage is about acknowledging, appreciating, accepting, and allowing events in our lives to happen. I described my experience of rappelling with the team earlier in the book. I was scared and vulnerable until I took the first step, and taking that first step was about trusting the person who was guiding me down the steep slope. He was my secure base.

Vulnerability is authenticity

Being authentic means being ready to express who we are and embrace the consequences. We are all searching for connection, and our brains need it. Deep, genuine connection is what we desire. Connection is often the missing piece of the puzzle that we are trying to solve. In truth, we sometimes doubt every piece in the puzzle, due to the many false fronts or facades we encounter daily. Do we have to continue to doubt every piece of the puzzle, or can we establish authentic connection by being vulnerable? Vulnerability is the invisible connection.

Vulnerability comes with loads of doubt and resistance, but it is a journey of power in our lives. If you allow yourself to experience vulnerability, you will feel uncomfortable. But that only lasts until you take your first step towards being authentic, and move towards your true self. Authenticity is about being heard, being seen, having difficult conversations, and genuinely speaking your mind. It is also about hearing your own voice and finding courage when you feel weak, or when the world is against you, or when being safe is not without cost. Authenticity is about taking action even when you are not sure of the outcome. If you focus authentically on your influence and impact within your circle, vulnerability will be your armour.

Are you comfortable with failure?

Most of us are not ready to fail. We fear the shame and guilt that comes with failure. We fear others' ridicule. The biggest saboteur in us is the judge who stops us from accepting failure as an integral part of success. The judge is critical and pushes us to do better without allowing us to fail. Learn to tell your judge to step aside. Life is about daring to be seen in the ring. Being ready to face challenges and problems in life is a boon. Being comfortable in the grey zone means being aware that you are facing the unknown, but believing that you will find your way and that the experience will be good for you as a whole person. For the judge inside us, we will never be good enough, but if we don't attempt to do what we fear, we will never know if we are good enough or not.

I am indebted to Henry Mouvillier, my boss at L'Oréal, who saw me struggling with wanting to do things right and recognised my low tolerance for failing to achieve what had been charted. He told me that it was important to risk failure and try things and be diligent in my approach. What follows is the result, and there is nothing right or wrong about it. *To achieve our goals, we have to stay open to change throughout the journey.*

I remember as I went home after my first meeting with Sunil Mittal, when he had spent a good hour and a half to present his vision for Airtel. While he was speaking of his vision with deep passion, I saw my purpose. I was thinking of the A-ha! moment when I found my purpose – *to change the way the average Indian lives*. I had my fears, and my judge was telling me that this goal was too big for me and that if I failed the world would laugh at me and ridicule me and I would lose all the respect I had earned in my career. In that internal debate, I remember telling my judge that this was the opportunity of a lifetime and that such opportunities do not come knocking every day. I told myself that I should take the opportunity and if I failed, I would be OK, as having tried and failed was better than not having tried at all. I had to focus on my experience, rather than what my critics might say.

Disrupt yourself, keep learning

Recognise your s curves and disrupt yourself to move ahead

Don't be afraid to jump from one curve to another

Start learning new skills before you start plateauing on your existing ones.

It calls for courage . Staying in your comfort zone is easy, but to succeed You need to be mobile

Find ways towards early Learning of skills & knowledge

I am not an engineer by education and this was what my judge kept reminding me. In my meeting with Sunil, I was impressed with his knowledge of the mobile telecom industry. I knew that, like me, he was not an engineer by education. So, if he could learn so much, then surely I could. The next five or more years were transformational. I sought opportunities to regularly challenge and disrupt myself. I realised that the S curve lifecycle of brands and companies also applied to our career lifecycles. This insight came easily to me as I had done this early in my life.

Every S curve represents a phase in your life. On each S curve, we need to reinvent ourselves before we plateau and start the downward slope. We need to read the indicators and step outside our comfort zone to jump from one S curve to the next. It's better to disrupt yourself when you have some control, rather than get disrupted by others.

During my career, I have taken this as a strategy for my career moves. As a student completing my MBA, I decided to major in Finance, even though I had not previously studied it. If I was to become a good Managing Director, it was essential for me to understand finance. This was the first time I consciously disrupted myself.

After working in finance for five years, I moved into the Marketing and Sales department of the company. P&G was my real B School where I learned to build and manage brands. I had jumped to another S curve. Four years later I left P&G to join a greenfield project to set up operations for L'Oréal in India. It was not easy. It was risky, as we operated through a franchisee for the first two years before the wholly-owned subsidiary was established. During my time at L'Oréal, I went back to a university program at INSEAD spread over 18 months. Seven years into the project, I realised that I wasn't on track to achieve my goal of becoming a Managing Director by the age of 40. I had to challenge my belief that MDs are groomed from within the company, and I jumped to the next S curve to become the MD for Gillette as an outsider. Working with a new team as an MD was a major disruption. In hindsight, every major decision was the start of a new S curve. Henry Mouvillier had taught me that it was important to stay in the grey zone and be ready to face change. This attitude made my career.

While I was the MD of Gillette, I was hit by a mid-life crisis and kept asking myself what I was doing in life. Did I have any impact on society? Was I doing anything to improve people's lives? As an industry leader, was I doing enough for society? That's when I met Sunil Mittal and found my purpose. That purpose gave me the confidence to disrupt myself again to join an unknown tech company. Then, at fifty, I quit industry to start a strategic consulting firm. Since then, I have downsized the firm to focus on Executive Coaching and have learned new ways of thinking and communicating. Over a lifetime, disrupting myself to learn, unlearn, and relearn, has become an enjoyable process.

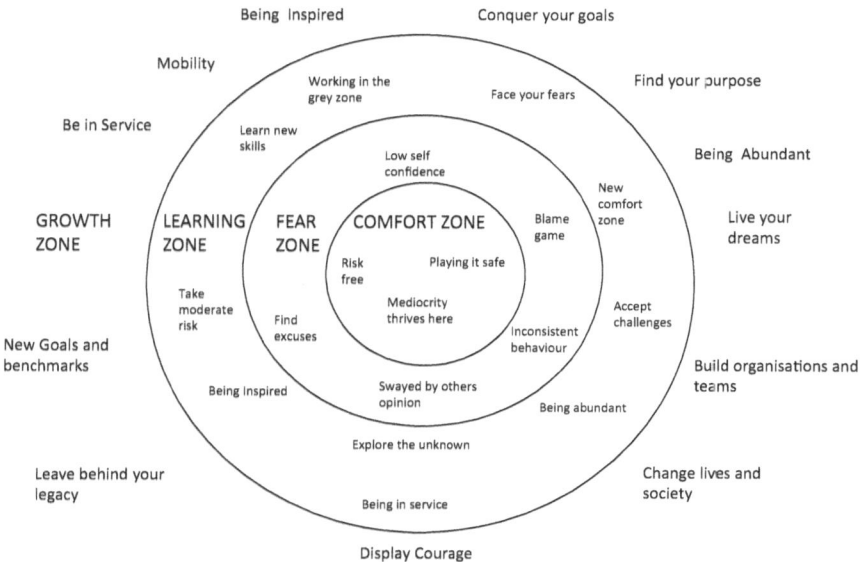

If you want to achieve your goals you must build a mindset of vulnerability and disruption. Staying in your comfort zone will ensure that you continue doing more of the same. The best thing about overcoming fear is that fear lasts only until you take the first step. But if you stay in your comfort zone to avoid failure, you will stagnate and slide on the downslope of the S curve, giving up on your goals and your aspirations. Initially, you might play the blame game and hold other people and situations responsible for your failure and frustration. You might not even be aware when you begin to display victim behaviour.

To get out of your comfort zone you need to face your fears. Fears are real, but with courage, you can face them head-on. One strategy that has helped me is to ask, "What is the worst-case scenario?" The judge in you will even remind you of similar experiences in the past to convince you to stay where you are. Please remember that *the past does not dictate your future.* Also, remember that other people's opinion comes from their own experiences. Fears may be keeping you from the experience of a lifetime. If you face your fears with courage, you will find yourself ready to learn and explore opportunities that you may not have considered. Arriving in this growth zone is akin to feeling the early morning sun, exuding soothing comfort and warmth. The growth zone is forgiving and offers you abundance.

When you keep learning you will not be aware of your entry into the growth zone. The two zones of learning and growth are interdependent and feed each other in a symbiotic relationship. The more you learn, the more you experience and test the learning and the more you grow. The growth zone offers you opportunities in abundance and offers you the opportunity of a lifetime to *be abundant.* What is *being abundant*?

10

BEING ABUNDANT

"When you are grateful, fear disappears and abundance appears."

— Tony Robbins

Doing what you love is perhaps the best expression of abundance in your life. To feel the abundance truly and deeply, we need to express gratitude for everything we have and receive. When a friend of mine visited her husband in the USA, they were invited to dinner at his sister's place. After dinner, her husband thanked his sister for the dinner. What struck my friend was that he had not ever thanked her for cooking him dinner at home. When I heard this, I realised that I had made that same mistake and immediately took corrective action after I heard her story. It is these small gestures that build a mindset of abundance.

Think abundance

How many times have you told yourself, "I wish I had more time", or, "If only I had the money to buy that dream house," or, "I wish I had that dream job"? Have you thought about the effect of such thinking on your system? *If only* thinking damages your mindset. It takes you away from your goals and attracts negativity as you feel stuck in a scarcity mindset and start to believe that you have no choice. This belief brings in the fear factor and limits the activity of the prefrontal brain and your thinking capacity. This scarcity mindset also has an impact on your relationships. We may be pushed or coerced to accept less than what we want, only to prove we are more than capable. After that, it is a catch-up process. So, can we change scarcity thinking to thinking abundance?

Thinking abundance is a mindset that focuses on what you have and on what you believe is yours, including happiness, joy, wealth, and success. Thinking abundance is about future possibilities. The mindset helps us open ourselves to being more resilient and creative, and to be in the speed of presence and our most productive self. Thoughts of "I can't" or "You are not" are to be viewed as saboteurs and a prompt to consciously move to sage thoughts of "I can" and "I will". In the abundance mindset, we can use feed-forward if we start to feel stuck. Feed forward is a process where you express your aspirations to your stakeholders and well-wishers and ask for suggestions. Listen to the suggestions and simply thank them for sharing their thoughts. No debates, please! List the suggestions and reflect on them to evaluate and move forward with your own decisions.

In a scarcity mindset, we tend to see competition, friends, and those who have what we want, as threats. We begin to believe that there isn't enough in the world and that we need to get what they have. To move from scarcity to sage thoughts is to believe that there is enough of everything in this world and this universe can feed us all. The next step is to truly celebrate other people's success. Believe that these people are showing the way, or have created pathways or proof of concept for you to follow. You can make successful people your learning models and understand what they did right to get there. Is it confidence, is it Openness, is it being authentic? What is success? And what does success feel like? Write it down to learn more as you proceed in your journey.

It is important to have faith and belief in your abilities and the goal you are working towards. You may find that once you have achieved a goal you are soon back where you started in terms of happiness. The key in your quest is to define how much is *enough*. At the age of fifty when I decided to hang up my boots in industry, many people told me that I was making a mistake. What guided me was my understanding of *enough*. I had to imagine what was enough for my current and future needs. Do I have financial freedom for the future? I just had to define the future lifestyle I wanted and the decision became easy.

Abundance is giving

As a young student, I never had enough pocket money. I always carried a 10 rupee note in my wallet to give me a sense of abundance and a safety net. To build an abundance mindset is to stay away from a scarcity mindset where we pay more attention to what we lack than what we have. Make a list of all that you have and are grateful for and you will realise how blessed you are. Reminding yourself of all that you have, and recognising that "more" will never fill you up, will allow you to appreciate how privileged you are.

I learned my lessons about abundance from nature. It is not that there are no problems, it is not that the problems are not real. We all have challenges. We all need to find our own solutions to our problems. But nature has taught me to look at the positives in the situation. Every time a BUT appears in the solution, I remind myself that nature has no buts, it stays the path of abundance and follows the path of giving.

I have been always fascinated by nature and its laws. The natural order and its patterns are there for us to marvel at. As a child, my visits to the Hoode beach at Kemmanu were fascinating. I would understand and experience the concepts of persistence, energy, creating your path, and discipline at a deeper level later in life. At the age of 8, when I asked my grandfather how he was so sure that rice would grow in the fields, his simple answer was that if you sow rice you will reap rice. He explained the agricultural process to me, describing how for a good crop you need good inputs. This was my first exposure to a simple equation that has served me well in life. *The output is completely dependent on the input.* This sounds very simple to follow until you try to control the inputs to get the desired output. Nature has no limits for giving and remains the best example of abundance.

Gratitude helped my relationships grow

I have learnt from my 4 years old grandson Kabir, the son of my daughter Anushree, that gratitude needs to be expressed every time and with consistency. Kabir is encouraged to say his thank you prayer every night before going to bed. Once I asked him who he had thanked last night and he said, "I said thank you to Grandma because she loves me very much". What an attitude this kid is teaching me.

Gratitude, for me, is a state of mind. Am I grateful to myself? I am grateful for my body, spirit, soul, and mind. I am grateful and I appreciate my thoughts. I accept all of my thoughts. I accept, approve and appreciate myself. Life loves me. I feel blessed to live the life that I am living in. Gratitude is not simply felt, but must be expressed for its full benefits to be experienced. I certainly feel the benefits of expressing gratitude to others. Expressing gratitude taps into our reserve of positive energy. It is as though we dip into our balance, but somehow on expressing gratitude our balance of positive energy becomes higher, not lower. I have not been able to express gratitude to myself. If I accomplish something difficult, I feel good, I feel confident, my status might rise, and I feel renewed with energy and knowledge, but I don't feel gratitude, or is that gratitude? Through experience, I have realised that we feel and express gratitude externally. When we are at the speed of presence and feel gratitude, it is often expressed as appreciation. This could be our family, friends, the company we work for, nature, or even the Almighty. We have much to be grateful for.

If we make an inventory of what we have, we will realise that we have more to be grateful for than what we lack. How many of us are grateful when we open our eyes in the morning for yet another day to express ourselves? If we don't feel grateful for another day, we are forgetting our blessing. If we count all our blessings, we will feel deep gratitude. Embracing gratitude is more than a positive feeling. In gratitude, we can express kindness and love, we feel energetic, happy and alive, and we sleep well and develop a stronger immune system. All these benefits from being grateful! Isn't it a beautiful equation?

Gratitude is the path to a higher level

Gratitude leads you to a higher level of awareness. It gives the fuel to propel you to your goals. In my early forties, I was the Managing Director of a multinational company and, by any standard, a successful executive. I was doing well and yet I felt a void inside me. I was grateful for what I had achieved, I had a beautiful family to go home to, and I could afford the luxuries in life. So, why the void? It came from being grateful. I thanked the Lord for what I had and was also giving back in my own way. The question which kept me awake at night, though, was "Am I doing enough?" Always, I got the answer that I was doing all I could for my team, my company and my family. Was I doing enough for society? That was the void. I needed the job and the salary, so I was in search of answers. I energised my goals and the reticular activation system (RAS) in my brain helped me look for opportunities. Then, the forces in the universe came together and presented me with the opportunity to meet Sunil Mittal. It was in that meeting that I found a new purpose in my work.

The move to Airtel enabled me to grow into a higher way of being. I shed emotional baggage and felt like a hot air balloon with no weights attached. I found a new pair of wings. At Airtel, the environment of freedom I experienced, the relationships I enjoyed, and the practices we adopted as a team, helped me evolve to become a better leader and closer to who I wanted to be. The disruption of the change was worth every twinge of stress and fear of failure. It's easy to connect the dots in the past with hindsight, but when you want to connect the dots in the future, your belief is the glue.

> *Imagine your career taking flight like a hot air balloon. What if there were weights attached to it? Can you generate the momentum and propulsion you need?*

Propulsion- that which moves you forward.
The desire, will, intention and energy to grow.
Open mind and compassion in the heart .
Emergence of your true self. / Spiritual Practices. (morning hour)
Action, divine intelligence and Transformation practices
Healing work on your gravity.
Being Inspired/ Abundant/ and in Service
Moving into the Learning and Growth zones.

Personal Gravity –that which holds you back from growing in to who you are at essence.
Limiting or false beliefs. / Self images
Fears and anxieties.
Ego patterns and self protection patterns.
Harmful behaviours and addictions.
Disempowering thought patterns./ Unattended sorrow.
Pain trauma and abuse.
Unresolved psychological and emotional issues.

Learning from Leon Vanderpol

The energy that propels you further comes from your desire and the clarity of your goals. Clear goals are a secure base that help you to disrupt yourself and move out of your comfort zone to learn and grow. We gain energy to propel us by keeping an open mind to all possibilities, a desire to serve, a belief in abundance, and the knowledge that we need to take care of our world. Deep gratitude and compassion for the planet help to top up these energy levels.

What holds you back are the fears you are not ready to face. Your limiting self-beliefs will also hold you back. Negative thoughts and scheming to pursue a personal agenda ahead of what is right are also headwinds in your journey. A lack of respect for people and relationships, or not honouring your commitments, are also weights that will hold down the hot air balloon of your journey. Every day, your actions either propel you forward or work against you. To be propelled, you must focus and be present.

Abundance made me courageous

My move to Airtel helped me change my mindset from scarcity to abundance. I had much to do, share, give, and learn. I had experienced many different shades of vulnerability in the past, but at Airtel, I began to view vulnerability as a strength. I was not afraid to say, "I don't know, let's find the answer together." Newfound courage dawned on me, and I began to understand courage at a deeper level. I saw courage as acknowledging, appreciating, accepting and allowing the events that we want to happen in our lives. I wanted to build a formidable team that would not be afraid to take up challenges and think and do things differently. *The most effective way to learn the art of tuning in to others is to attune to your own inner self.* At Airtel, for every answer I sought for the outside, I began to go inside. This stirring of my inner self burst into a statement I made when addressing the Maharashtra and Goa circle team, "A song in your heart, a twinkle in your eye, and a smile on your face makes the world a beautiful place."

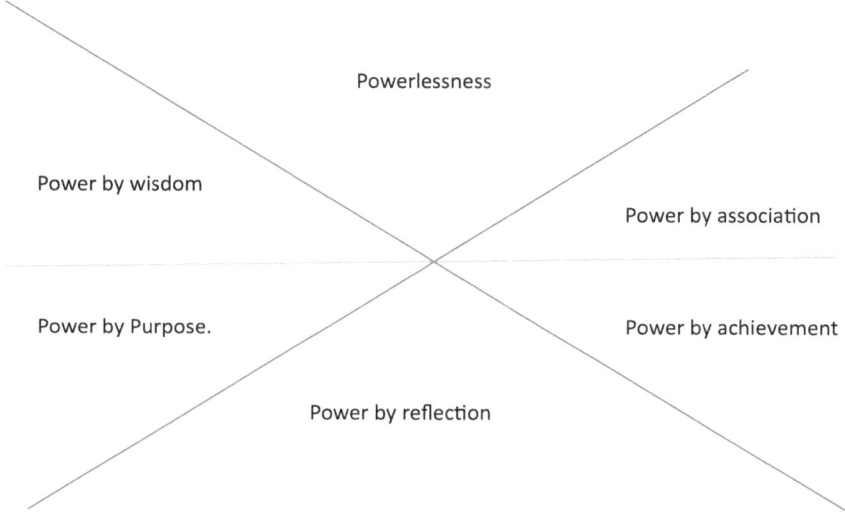

From the book Real power - Stages of personal power in Organizations by Janet Hagberg

This model gave me a feeling of having witnessed the different powers in a chronological order from childhood to youth to maturity, as though it represented personal development over their lifetime. Today, I use different powers at different times.

The ability to influence followers is a function of a leader's power. As leaders, we draw from the power of our past successes. These achievements give us strength and confidence to move ahead and strategize. In our youth, we took pride in associations that gave us our sense of identity. As leaders, we take help from our network to resolve issues or manage situations. My inner voice kept reminding me of my responsibility to use my power wisely. While my power from achievement was high, I was driven by my power of purpose, guided by my power of wisdom, and leading through my power of reflection. The power of purpose is the most understated and the least understood source of Power. Purpose helps us to find meaningful solutions and helps us adopt clear and simple strategies to execute tasks. My purpose to "changing the way an average Indian lives" helped us build a 2-billion-dollar company in a matter of five years.

Abundance is expressed in many different ways

What I learnt from my manager at P&G, Keki Pardiwala, I experienced at Airtel. Keki spent twelve nights in the office with his team when P&G acquired RHL in India as there was a deadline to submit audited books of accounts. At Airtel, we were going through a brand logo change and our TV commercial was to be released. The morning newspaper would carry a full-page advertisement.

On the morning of the day before we were scheduled to launch the new brand logo with all its fanfare, Gautam Mukherjee came to me and said that the skins for the hoardings would not be ready for the brand logo launch the next morning. People would see the old logo on the hoardings after the TV commercial had aired, and the new brand campaign would be suboptimal. This mismatch was not acceptable. We had to change the skins on the hoardings that evening so that the hoardings would feature the new design the next morning to match the newspaper advertisement. My response to Gautam was that we still had 24 hours to get it right.

That evening, I got home at 10 pm and as I ate dinner, I thought of the marketing team working on getting the new skins up. A quick phone update told me that the skins were ready and they would work through the night so that the new logo designs would be there by morning for customers to see. At 11 pm, I pulled out in my car and drove around the city to meet the team and express my gratitude. Realising at midnight that they hadn't had dinner, I called Stanley, our Admin manager. Apologising profusely for the late call, I explained to him that I need chilled beer and kebabs for the team who were working through the night. At 2.30 am we celebrated with chilled beer and kebabs. Thank you, Keki, for the gift.

I have been fortunate in my career with bosses like Mickey Dayal, Keki, Sumit Bhattacharya, Samar Mazumdar, Ravi Sivaraman, Henry Mouvillier, Jean Jacque Mason De Blaise, and Brandy Gill who protected me and gave me a sense of security throughout my career. They have been my secure base in the true sense. *Secure base* is a term I learnt from George Kohlrieser when I met him at Nashik. I was the coach for the Future Leadership Program and George had come to address the senior leadership team of Mahindra and Mahindra. More about secure base in the next chapter.

11

BE THE SECURE BASE

> "Let's not forget it's you and me VS the problem and NOT you VS me."
>
> — STEVE MARBOLI

The term *secure base* comes from the post-war attachment theory of John Bowlby and Mary Ainsworth. According to their theory, humans have an innate desire for closeness and comfort from someone who gives them a sense of protection and security. People without a secure base feel insecure and are looking for security. As a leader, do you go out of your way to make your team feel secure? Do you see it as part of your responsibility to make them feel secure? Is there a reason for this?

As we have learned, the brain's response to threat is flight or fight. Without a sense of security or a safety net, the brain will prompt a person to avoid risk and resist change whenever a threat is perceived. A safety net allows the person to respond positively, and see opportunity instead of threat. The person's focus shifts to positives such as learning, reward, opportunity, and experience.

I vividly remember watching a video of Ted Kennedy Jr giving a speech. He was talking about himself when he was young and had been diagnosed with bone cancer and lost a leg to the illness. Sometime later, the Kennedy family were in the country when heavy snow fell. Ted's father, Ted Kennedy Sr, asked Ted Jr if he'd like to go skiing. Ted Jr was just about getting used to his artificial leg. The hill they ventured out on was covered with ice and snow and it was not easy to walk. As Ted Jr tried to climb the hill, he struggled to keep his footing and slipped and fell. In tears, he told his father that he couldn't do it. Ted Kennedy Sr picked him up in his arms and said, "There is nothing you can't do. We are going to climb that hill together, even if it takes all day."

Another story that inspires me is that of Derek Anthony Redmond. A British 400m runner at the 1992 Barcelona Olympic Games, Redmond didn't win a medal. He didn't make it past the semi-finals. But his determination to finish will live on in the minds of millions. Injury had forced the Briton to withdraw from the 1988 Seoul Games just ten minutes before the start of his 400m heat. In Barcelona four years later, Redmond felt he had everything to prove.

At the start of the race, Redmond charged out of the blocks and made good speed over the first 250m. At that point, his right hamstring snapped. The one-time British 400m record holder pulled up as the rest of the field ran on, leaving Redmond on his knees. His Olympic dream was shattered. What followed was one of the most memorable moments in Olympic history. Redmond got back onto his feet to finish the race. He could only hop on one leg and pain was written all over his face, with each step more painful than the last. But he refused to give up. He had promised his father and himself that he would finish the race "no matter what," and he kept that promise.

Halfway to the finish line, on one leg and crying with pain, Derek was joined by his father Jim. When Redmond crossed the finish line, thousands of spectators were brought to their feet in a standing ovation.

Redmond's story reminded me of our inter-school athletics when I fell and did not complete the race. My coach, Mr Andrade, told me that it was my responsibility to finish the race, and I interpreted his words as *a lesson for life, to finish what I start.*

Just as Jim and Ted were the secure base for their sons, you are the secure base for your team. We understand that we are the secure base for our families, but we can have a similar attitude towards our team. A secure base inspires and brings energy to an individual. They help their team members take the first step out of their comfort zone. To be a secure base, one needs to first understand oneself as a person and as a leader. Mothers, fathers, grandparents, and other significant caregivers, are the first secure base we experience. As we grow up and experience the power of associations, we experience different kinds of protection and security and begin to understand what it means to be secure at a broader level.

As a leader of your team or company, one of your main responsibilities is to encourage your team members to present their best selves. Your energy must be contagious, to get your team to dip into their energy reserves to accomplish team goals. Being a secure base is about taking your team to previously unimaginable levels.

In *Care to Dare,* George Kohlrieser defined secure base leadership as

> *"The way a leader builds trust and influences others, by providing a sense of protection, safety and caring and by providing a source of inspiration that together produce energy for daring, exploration, risk-taking and seeking challenge."*

Who is a secure base leader?

For a leader to provide a sense of safety and caring, as well as being an inspiration who exudes contagious energy, sounds difficult and complex. Try breaking it down into simple behaviours. One of the fundamental characteristics of a secure base is to be *rock solid* in crises, remaining calm and displaying dependable behaviour. This is a leader who somehow "knows what to do when we don't know what to do". Being rock solid depends on listening with a deep intent to understand and empathise. Deep Listening skills will help you be at the speed of presence and your most productive self. Empathy will help you to understand the pressure your team members experience and their efforts to manage it. This may give you insights into motivators for the team to explore, and learnings that they could experience. Deep Listening will also help you to activate your *communication quotient* and use the *SCARF* model from your leadership toolkit.

A secure base leader sees every team member as a capable contributor. Besides acknowledging and accepting each team member, you go beyond that to see their potential. The secure base leader can see potential in every team member and will bring to conversations the belief that the team member is capable and will deliver. There is no doubt or baggage from the past. For this leader, the primacy of the individual overrides any specific issues. They relate to team members' dreams and aim to integrate them into the company vision. They take every opportunity to remind the team members and themselves of the vision they are working towards. They encourage risk-taking and present the team with opportunities to choose to disrupt themselves and take ownership of actions while being confident of their safety. Secure base leaders focus on encouraging team members to test their potential through intrinsic motivation, rather than for external rewards. Intrinsic motivation calls on a deep understanding of what team members love to do, truly allowing them to bring their passion and creativity to the table. Secure base leaders drive action and are focused on a positive future. They help the team visualise the benefits of the goal and direct their efforts towards the goal. In the process, they energise the team members' individual goals and build synergy that can drive exponential growth and results.

Secure base leaders help ordinary people become extra-ordinary.

My goal was my secure base

When I consider my goal of wanting to be the Managing Director of a multinational company by the age of 40, my focus for close to two decades, my goal was my secure base. Having that goal helped me to overcome resistance, and energised me to disrupt myself and step out of my comfort zone. George Kohlrieser explains that a relationship with any entity that enhances your inner sense of safety and inspires exploration can be a secure base. The stronger the secure base, the more resilient you will be in the face of adverse or stressful circumstances.

Everyone needs both people and goals as secure bases. Goals provide a sense of security that comes from knowing your destination with some certainty and challenge you to strive for greater achievement.

The words of Prof P C Narayan still ring in my ears. With the stress, pulls and pushes of a career, it is tempting to move the goalposts away from your main goal to what looks more achievable and would still be awesome in the eyes of others. It is very easy to rationalise that becoming VP of Marketing and Sales is a very successful career in itself. If your goal was to become Managing Director, you might let it go when you realise what needs to be done to achieve that goal. If you feel like moving the goalposts to something easier, ask yourself what it would feel like to be moving forward? What would it feel like the day you are appointed as the Managing director of the company?

Moving forward means making decisions. Decisions compel you to take action. Many of us do not see the opportunities in life, simply because opportunities come dressed in overalls. Opportunities are hard work. They might bring disruption and risks, they might involve learning a new skill. Taking decisions that propel you forward is hard for many of us as it represents change, and many people find change hard to accept. That's why more than three-quarters of us stay in our comfort zone.

David Wethey in *Decide – Better Ways of Making Better Decisions*, suggested that:

> "Winning or losing in both business and life often depends on making a decision – and making the right one is obviously preferable, but it is usually better to make a decision and live with it, than delay indefinitely. After all, we learn through taking risks and can't expect to be right all the time."

This reminds me of a manager that I had fired, to fire him up. After I fired him, his career took an upward trajectory. This kind of wake-up call can come from anywhere. Do we wait for a fire to be lit under us or are we willing to do it ourselves? The harsh reality is that the only person holding you back is yourself. You are holding yourself hostage. You are bound and entangled with your limiting beliefs and fears, and it is easy to feel paralysed. Energise yourself with the vision of your goal. For years, I visualised myself driving a big, expensive car to a swanky office complex to attend a Board meeting.

Visualisation empowered me

It is important to visualise the end picture of the goal as the brain is visual and we often think through images. The image of me in my car energised my goal daily and helped to activate my reticular activation system and identify opportunities. This image was the secure base that guided me forward through my career.

Staying the course of your goal is not easy. Meaningful, valuable goals require dedication, sacrifice, and discipline. There will be times when you need to test your potential. You will never understand your potential until you test its limits, and then you will often be surprised at what you are capable of. ASK Rangan, my friend Girish's father, who was then the Chief Human Resources Officer of Colgate Palmolive, gave me some valuable advice. I met him when I was nervous and scared about taking on the challenge of setting up L'Oréal in India. He told me, "Take it up to prove to yourself that you are a good leader."

Many of us live in the past or the future and lose the experience of the now. We are at our productive best at the speed of presence. We can't change the past, so what use is it to live in the past? When we live in the past, the emotion we experience is regret for what we could have done. This attitude depletes our balance of positive energy and leads us to miss current opportunities, taking away from what needs to be done in the now to move forward. If we consistently dwell on the past, we risk developing limiting beliefs that will hold us hostage. Rather than dwelling on our past mistakes and failures as the opposite of success, we need to acknowledge them as a part of success. Mistakes are learning opportunities, and if it was not for this learning, most successful people would not have achieved what they have. When you embrace setbacks, you will better appreciate yourself and brace yourself for the journey ahead.

While it is true that our beliefs shape our actions, the plasticity of our brains and our drive to adapt to new situations mean we can rewire our brains and change our behaviour. If you've struggled with change in the past, now is the time to embrace it. Accept change and rewire.

There is no perfect time to begin the change. The right time is now. All success stories are made up of small, incremental steps. The first step is the beginning of a new habit. As a form of disruption, change creates new insights as the brain works to find a new certainty. Change is about being in the grey zone. Try to talk to yourself about the certainty in uncertain situations. In every uncertain situation, there is a line between the amount of uncertainty that is manageable, and the amount of uncertainty that is too much. Focus on the boundaries and see how your brain responds to uncertainty. When you take the first step into the grey zone, does it become certain?

BE THE SECURE BASE

Accountable behaviour propelled me

I was as scared as hell every time I disrupted myself. When I chose to major in Finance for my MBA, when I moved from Finance to Marketing and Sales in P&G, when I joined L'Oréal as a start-up in India, or when I joined Airtel with little knowledge about the company. In hindsight, every decision was beneficial and helped me move forward to achieve my cherished goal. Every step I took increased my self-belief and self-esteem and raised my status to a level where I could focus on the positives and see the benefits for the team.

Self-Awareness and self-belief are the foundations of success. Success is about taking ordinary moments and making them extraordinary. It is about seizing those moments and working to make the outcome memorable and epic.

If you wish to step into your *Power of Achievement,* then commit to moving forward. Commit to the first step that will take you on a journey to your *Power of Reflection* and *Power of wisdom.* Display accountable behaviour.

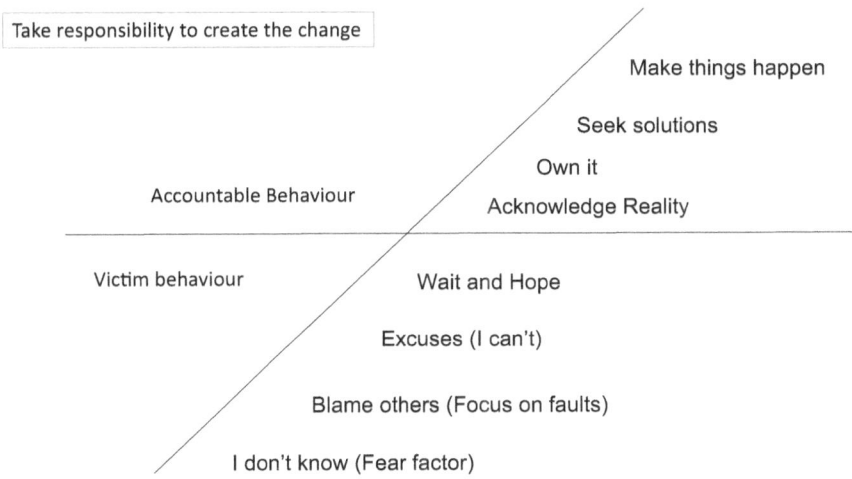

Take responsibility for your life and goals. Take responsibility for moving forward and taking action. Victim behaviour makes you focus on blaming others for what has not worked for you. Research has found that people who display victim behaviour feel sorry for themselves and have difficulty expressing and processing negative emotions such as anger, fear, and disappointment. These people often fail to take responsibility for their actions and decisions. Move away from the *Power of Helplessness*. As a child, you were helpless as you had no resources. As an adult, visualise the benefits of managing the situation to help change your frame from victim to accountability.

Keep in mind that personal growth doesn't happen overnight. There is no magic potion to take. Growth is a process. We all want growth and we never stop growing. The moment we appreciate that our journey is towards actualising our potential, personal growth becomes rewarding.

Learn to embrace learning. A growth mindset will help you achieve goals and create a life filled with opportunities. In the words of Eric Butterworth, *"Don't go through life; grow through life."*

If you aren't moving forward, you aren't stationary, you're moving backwards. To move forward, you may think you need to have a coach. Yes, every one of us has a coach within us. You just need to listen deeply. You could also be a two-minute coach to every person you interact with. Sounds easy? It is, as you will see in the next chapter.

12

BE THE TWO-MINUTE COACH

"Just because people understand what to do doesn't ensure that they will actually do it."

— Marshall Goldsmith

Before we go any further, I ask you to be a coach leader. Lead your team members through the coaching process. With great insight, Marshall Goldsmith summed it up beautifully: coaching is a tool to get your team to move from understanding to action.

Well, what is coaching? A good definition of professional coaching could be:

> *"A one-to-one relationship wherein a professional coach assists an individual in gaining increased self-awareness (strengths and weaknesses) and developing significant insights and abilities (new knowledge and skills) to enhance work performance (results) and personal satisfaction."*

The essence of executive coaching is helping team members get unstuck from dilemmas and find the way forward. Executive coaching is about guiding a team to think differently, dive deep into their experience and knowledge, and translate it into results that will advance the organisation.

A coach is focused on the future. Unlike counselling, coaching focuses on the present and the will to move forward through action. Where a mentor shares domain knowledge, a coach asks questions to encourage discovery. Where a consultant offers advice, a professional coach would resist advice-giving and instead guide the team member to think their way through to the solution and to own it. As a leader, you wear the different hats of consultant, mentor, or coach but, in my experience, it is the coach that is most effective for getting your team members to be fully engaged in solutions, and for those solutions to be the best outcomes. The diagram maps out the difference between coaching and other interventions.

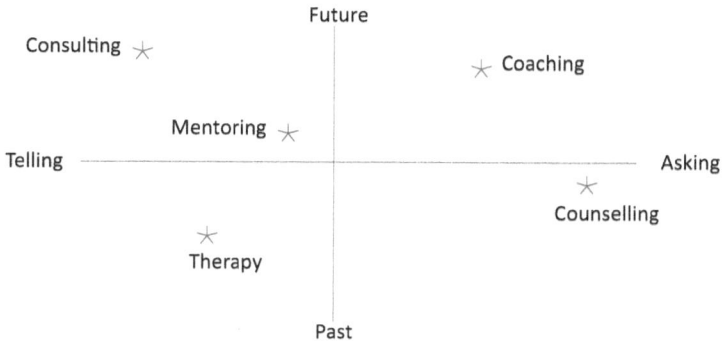

Some leaders that I have coached have thought of coaching their teams as additional work. It's not. All I am asking you to do is rethink the way you communicate. Let's say you are the leader and one of your team members has returned from an important client meeting. We tend to ask, "How did the meeting go?" *Hold it there and change the communication.*

Let's take a look at a coaching conversation.

Coach leader. Hey, I'm sure the meeting went well. What are the chances of us closing the deal?

Team member. Yes, it went well and I'd say our chances are maybe 80% of closing the deal.

Coach leader. Well, what is needed from our side to make it 100%? What do you need and from whom? Can you write up a one-page summary?

Team member. Yes, I'll work on it.

Coach leader. When do you think you can share the summary with us? And do let me know what help you might need.

This 2-minute interaction made the team member think, commit, and take ownership of the steps that need to be actioned. Look at the coaching process using the SCARF model:

1. Has it raised the team member's Status?
2. Has it created Certainty?
3. Has it offered Autonomy to your team member?
4. Has it increased Relatedness?
5. Have you been a Fair leader?

To take your team from good to great, being a coach leader could make the difference. Your effectiveness as a coach leader will depend on the quality of the team culture, which depends on the quality of team relationships, which depends on the quality of conversations. Conversations are energising, help us form bonds, and help us discover.

Discover through questions

Add your own questions to the examples based on Judith Glaser's work:

Current situations

- Let's understand the situation, what are the facts?
- Who (which departments) is impacted by this situation?

Understanding feelings and insights

- What issues concern you? What do you fear might happen?
- How can we build trust in this situation?

Sharing experiences and insights

- Would you like to share your experience with this situation?
- Does anyone see the facts in a different light?
- What is your attention on now?

Exploring ideas

- Would you like to share your idea with us?
- What do you wish to achieve with this idea?

Exploring vision

- What is your vision of success? What is our desired outcome?
- What opportunities do we see?

Creating insights

- How can we build on each other's ideas to combine them into a formidable strategy?
- What do we need to do to get the best outcome?

Possibilities

- If there are no constraints, what are the possibilities?
- What if everybody in the room was pushing for this? What would the result be?

Creating perspectives

- If we have the resources for a significant breakthrough, what would it be?
- If you were in their shoes, how would you see the issue?
- If a customer was watching us now, what would they think?

Provoking thoughts

- To whom are you addressing that question?
- What do you want to allow here?
- What do we want to create?

Putting assumptions on the table

- What assumptions do you hold about this strategy?
- What would it be like if your assumptions were not true? Are we missing anything?

Generating ideas

- What is good about this situation? Do we see any opportunities?
- What must we do to make this happen?

Team development is my responsibility

Teamwork is essential for achieving any goal. There is something magical about getting a group of people to align in thought and action. Often, this can be daunting or overwhelming. In my experience, when teamwork is lacking the core issue is whose responsibility it is to align the team. You might believe it is everyone's responsibility, but as a coach leader, I found it was my responsibility.

As a coach leader, remember you are leading development at two levels: organisational development, and the personal development of team members. Without personal impact, the impact on the organisation will be limited. Your team members are always looking to you for consistency, and while this has the deepest impact at the personal level, its impact flows into the culture of the organisation. If your energy is contagious, you can energise the team. If you are ready to walk the talk, you will see the team doing the same.

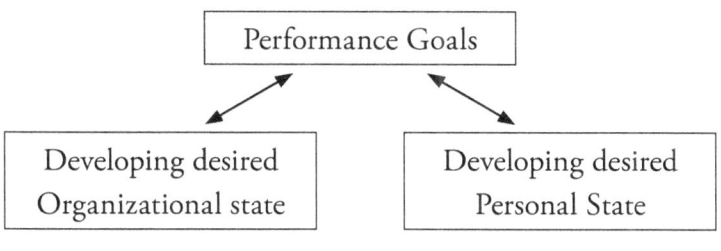

Communication systems   Leadership skills
Organisational culture   Personal skill set
Social capital   Communication skills
Strategy   Energy levels/commitment

As a 2-minute coach, focus on building the personal development of team members, and you will create awareness of the desired organisational state. Your focus needs to be felt in every interaction with every team member.

You are a subset of the system

As a coach leader, be aware of the team dynamics that include you, your team, and the organisation's system. The system influences you and the team, and you and the team influence each other, and influence the system.

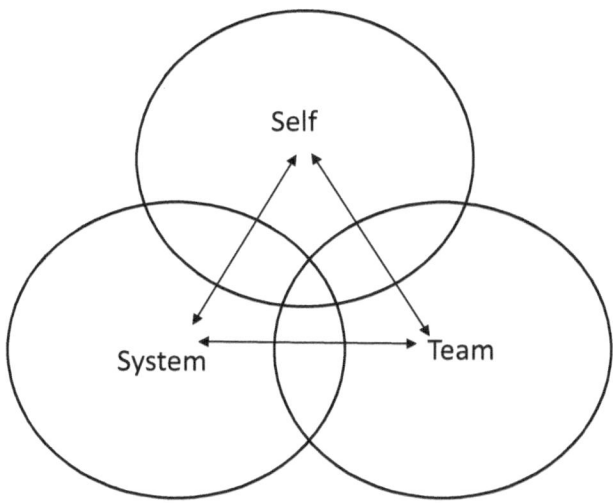

Create an environment where every individual is willing to go within themselves to look for solutions for the organisation. The most coachable members of your team may already be self-directed, insightful, motivated learners, committed to their development. They may rarely need a coach, but you can encourage them to be *change agents* who create awareness and contribute to a culture of creative thinking and leadership. Whether team members are coachable or not often depends on the coach leader's ability. You don't need to be a trained coach – Judith Glaser's CQ and David Rock's SCARF provide all the tools you need. Be at the speed of presence and remember that your presence is felt not by what you say but by how you make your team feel. How your team feels depends on how you communicate.

It's all about facilitating change through improved thinking

Being a coach leader is more effective than consulting, mentoring, or advising. Team members get ready for personal change through the insights they discover through powerful questioning.

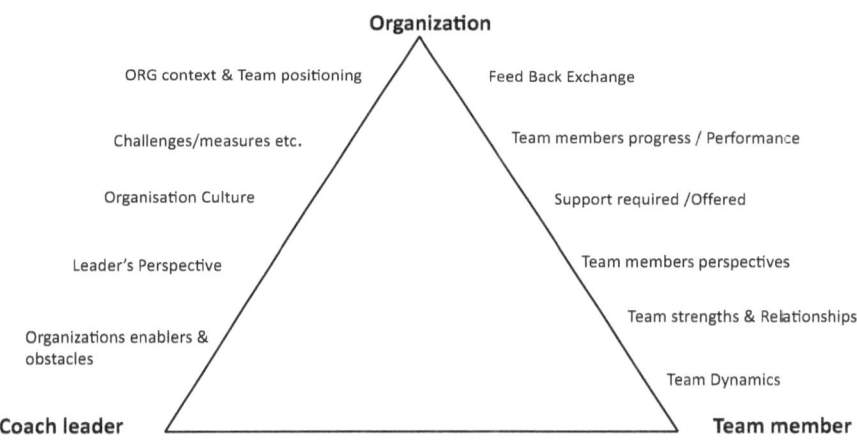

Coaching Conversations, Creating Insights, Feed-Forward, SCARF, Measurements (XL Sheets)

Tips for coaching conversations

1. Start interactions with the assumption that the team member is capable and will deliver what is needed.
2. Ask open-ended questions. *How could we improve on this?*

3. Ask questions that challenge assumptions. *Can you talk a bit about what your assumptions are in this case?*
4. Ask questions to encourage your team member to clarify their goal and move into action mode. *What are we trying to achieve? What could the next step be?*
5. Offer feedback. Feedback given with utmost transparency and honesty will always go down well. Effective feedback can raise the recipient's status. Give *feed-forward*, acknowledging what has been done well. *Seek permission before giving feedback.*
6. Encourage team members to practise awareness. Encourage role-plays and create scenarios to rehearse the new behaviours that emerge from team members' insights. Follow up on the changes team members attempt to make and use feed-forward to drive change. When people know there will be a follow up, they will find ways to deliver.
7. Encourage and schedule off-site gatherings with no agenda, to allow the team to reflect together.
8. Talk consistently about creating awareness and use the *GROW* (Goals, current Reality, Opportunities, Way forward) model. This model has always worked for me.
9. Look at each member of the team as a person who could replace you and construct a developmental plan for each. Your objective is to build a robust leadership bench for the organisation. It is important to take a coach-like approach with conviction, based on evidence that it works for the good of organisations. If you believe in the journey, you will sustain a long-term focus and will soon see the benefits.

Build teams the coaching way

Another gem from Marshall Goldsmith:

> *"Teams built by Coach Leaders have strong bonds and work better as the belief in each other is deep-rooted. Improvement in teamwork tends to occur when team members develop their own behavioural change strategies rather than just executing a change strategy that has been imposed upon them by the "boss"."*

Step 1. Begin by asking all members of the team to confidentially record their answers to two questions on a scale from 1 (not at all well) to 10 (ideal):
  1. How well are we doing in terms of working together as a team?
  2. How well do we need to be doing in terms of working together as a team?

Step 2. Have a team member calculate the results. Discuss the results with the team. If team members believe that the gap between current and needed effectiveness indicates a need for team-building, proceed to the next step. In most cases, team members believe that improved teamwork is both needed and important. In interviews of hundreds of teams from multinational corporations, the "average" team member believed their team was functioning at 5.8/10 in effectiveness and needed to be at 8.7/10.

Step 3. Ask the team members what they would try to change if they could change two key behaviours to help close the gap between where they are and where they want to be. Have each team member record their chosen behaviours.

Step 4. Help the team prioritise the behaviours they have identified as a group and determine, by consensus, the most important behaviour to change for the team as a unit.

Step 5. Have team members hold a series of five-minute, one-on-one conversations with each team member and suggest two areas for personal behaviour change that could help the team close the gap, in addition to the one already identified. Hold the dialogues simultaneously, much like the feed-forward format. For example, 'please help me identify two behaviours you think I need to focus on for better team productivity'.

Step 6. Let team members review their list of suggested personal behaviour changes and choose the one they think is most important. Have team members share their key behaviour for personal change with the team. As a team we now have one behaviour chosen by the team to focus on, and one behaviour for each team member chosen by themselves to focus on.

Step 7. Encourage team members to organise brief (five-minute) monthly meetings with team members to ask for three "suggestions for the future" (feed-forward). Feed forward is where you ask your colleague for suggestions. You greet the person and state what you wish to achieve. E.g. I wish to demonstrate more patience, please help me with three suggestions. No discussions on the subject, please listen, record the suggestions and say Thank you. Encourage each member to reflect on the suggestions and their own efforts in the direction.

Step 8. Conduct a mini-survey six months later to follow up. Based on the mini-survey, provide each team member with a confidential feedback from the other team members about the effectiveness of their behaviour change.

Sample mini-survey

For each item, use the scale from 1 (no change) to 4 (appreciable change) to indicate whether this team member has become more or less effective in the past six months. Circle the number that best matches your estimate of the change in effectiveness.

Team Behaviour

   1. e.g., Clarifies roles and expectations with fellow team members
   1- No change, 2- Small change making an effort, 3- Visible change 4- Appreciable Change

Individual Behaviour

   2. e.g., Genuinely listens to others
   1- No change, 2- Small change making an effort, 3- Visible change 4- Appreciable Change

Overall effective behaviour

3. Is an effective team member
1- No change, 2 – Small change making an effort, 3- Visible change 4- Appreciable Change
4. How frequently has this team member followed up with you about the areas they have been trying to improve? (Check one.)
no perceptible follow-up – a little – some – frequent – consistent (Periodic) follow-up
5. What can this individual do to become a more effective team member? (*Write your answer in the space below*)

Pre- and post-intervention studies have shown that when team members regularly follow up with colleagues, they are perceived to have increased in effectiveness. Individual reports from the mini-survey will provide an opportunity to positively reinforce team members' improvement, and gain insight into what may not have improved, after only a short period. The mini-survey will also reinforce the value and importance of "*sticking with it*" and "*following up.*"

Step 9. Calculate team members' results and calculate summary results for the group (on common team items). Share confidential individual summary reports with team members, and a summary report of the team's progress on items selected for all team members.

Step 10. In a team meeting, have each team member discuss key learnings from their mini-survey results and ask for further suggestions in brief one-on-one dialogues with every other team member.

Step 11. Review the summary results with the team. Facilitate a discussion about how the team as a whole is doing with increasing its effectiveness. Provide the team with positive recognition for increased effectiveness in teamwork. Encourage team members to keep focused on demonstrating the behaviours identified for improvement.

Step 12. Have every team member conduct brief monthly, progress conversations with every other team member. Every fourth months, re-administer the mini-survey.

Step 13. Conduct a summary session with the team one year after the exercises were begun. Review the results of the final mini-survey and ask team members to rate the team's effectiveness when working together as a team using the 1 (*not well*) to 10 (*ideal*) scale. Compare these ratings with the original ratings calculated a year earlier.

If team members follow the process reasonably closely, the team should anticipate a dramatic improvement in teamwork. Give the team positive recognition for improvement in teamwork and have each team member recognise improvements in the behaviour of each colleague in a brief one-on-one dialogue. Ask team members if they believe more work on team-building will be needed. If the team believes more work would be beneficial, continue the exercises. If not, celebrate and work on something else!

Why team-building works

These team-building exercises work because they are highly focused and include specific feedback, actions to take, and follow-up. The program is streamlined and brief, and the survey questionnaires are short and tailored to each team member's unique needs. The program is also effective as it provides ongoing feedback and reinforcement. Behaviour change theory is supported by research evidence that feedback and reinforcement of new behaviour need to occur more frequently than annually or bi-annually. The program also works because it encourages team members to focus on solving their own problems rather than someone else's!

I will close this chapter with a challenge to you as a team leader: Try it! There are very few downsides and the "upsides" are many. Effective teamwork is more and more important in the corporate world and the brief amount of time invested may bring great returns for you, your team, and your organisation.

I hope that after reading these chapters you have a keen interest to learn more and continue to practise your insights. Your learning won't be complete until it's been tested. Having worked on yourself, your team, and the people in your circle of influence, it's now time to create your future. When you try to predict the future from the known you're plotting a future that is more of the same. But when you work with the unknown, you're creating a different future. The unknown is the perfect place to start to create something new.

In the final chapters, I share my stories of creating the future.

13

DON'T PREDICT THE FUTURE, CREATE IT

"Instead of worrying about what you cannot control,
shift your energy to what you can create."

— Roy T. Bennett, The Light in the Heart.

We have reached the end of the book and I hope you have begun your journey to achieve your goals with new insight. In this chapter, I'll take you through two journeys – one, my personal goal, and the other, my purpose at Airtel. You'll find that in many ways these two journeys were more similar than different.

An important step in creating the future is to take stock of your current life and decide what you want to take into your new life, what you want to change, and what you want to strengthen. To create the future, we change the way we perceive the world around us, the way we feel, the way we think – our very biology. Yes, you will create a new you that only you can give shape to. What you have learnt from this book has put all the tools you need to create your new personal reality within your reach.

Goals and purpose

If there is one thing everyone in this world wants, it is GROWTH. The importance of having a goal to work towards cannot be stressed enough. Having purpose in pursuing our goals is part of human nature. Goals give us direction and every model of growth starts with a goal. Even a simple goal is better than no goal at all. You know where you want to go and this gives you the motivation and energy to get into action mode and map out your way there. Every success story is written twice. First, when you dream it, and then when you ACTION it.

When Prof. P C Narayan asked our class at B school to write down one or two specific goals we wanted to achieve in our lifetime, my goals were:

1. Be the Managing Director of a mid-sized multinational company by the age of forty.
2. Retire at the age of fifty.

I hadn't thought through my second goal, but I felt that ten years as an MD would be long enough to live out my goal, and then retirement would allow me to pursue other passions and new goals. I celebrated my forty-first birthday as MD at Gillette and forty-six days before I turned fifty was my last day at Airtel.

Your hunger to achieve your goal must be immense. Your desire to achieve will keep you awake at night and motivate you to do more than you thought you were capable of. Just as Prof P C Narayan told us there would be, there were times when I doubted myself. I had to face my doubts and fears and ask myself if I had strayed from the straight line. But I kept confidence in my goals by believing that I would achieve them and preparing myself for that day. That meant a lot of preparation over the sixteen-year journey. When I wrote my goal statement I promised myself that I would be an efficient and effective MD. Every day of these sixteen years I reminded myself of what I was preparing for. I regularly asked myself:

1. Am I happy doing what I am doing?
2. Is this what I want to continue doing?
3. Have I done enough to move towards my goal?
4. Am I close to the straight line?
5. What else do I need to prepare myself?

It was a constant quest to upgrade my skills. These questions made me restless but also made me think deep and face my fears. I had some sleepless nights but I did find my purpose and joined Airtel "to change the way an average Indian lives."

Energise the goals, visualise the benefits. You must have complete clarity in your goal. Our brains are visual and often understand images more clearly than language. Converting your goal statement into an end image will help you achieve it. Visualise the benefits of your goal and how you will celebrate achieving it. If you will celebrate with a family holiday at Disneyland, then that is the image that will energise your goal. If you wish to give up smoking, visualise excelling in the sport you play. Visualise every minor detail in the picture. For me, the picture was driving a car, parking it, and entering a swanky office where an energetic team was ready to win in the market. Remember the colour of the car, you may need it when you buy it.

At Airtel, my end picture was every Indian using their phone. A car driver talking on his mobile phone. Fishermen talking on their phones. The woman who managed our home affairs with her own mobile handset. These images were a secure base and gave me the strength to disrupt the structures within myself and build bold new strategies.

We networked with Nokia, Samsung, Ericson and others to increase their phones' distribution depth and reach and make them more affordable. Having this purpose helped me focus on expanding the pie with the belief that market share would follow. With this belief, I committed to much higher growth than the market rate as we were focused on expanding the market rather than leading it.

Research by psychologist Carol Dweck suggests two basic mindsets for how people think about their abilities: the fixed mindset and the growth mindset. People with a growth mindset are aware that the brain can change, hardwire new habits, and grow. People who believe in themselves and their capacity to grow are more likely to achieve success. When faced with difficult situations, they look for ways to improve their skills and keep working toward success.

> "I like to reinvent myself – it's part of my job."
>
> — Karl Lagerfeld

Disruptions helped me grow. In the sixteen years it took me to become a Managing Director, I knew one thing for sure: I was not ready and had to prepare myself to be worthy of the responsibility that

I was seeking. I built mental toughness to be ready to put in hard work and effort. I built belief in myself and my abilities. I cut out negative self-talk and looked for ways to stay positive and encourage myself. I had to be aware of the limiting beliefs I had and the ones that I might develop during the journey. I had to remind myself numerous times that other people had a right to their perspectives, but I didn't have to share them. I learned quickly that I needed to have a *bias for action*, as with every step forward my self-belief and confidence grew.

I designed simple strategies to reach my North Star. To prepare myself to be an MD, I had to put my strategies into action in the present – there was no tomorrow. It took disruption, time, and effort. At B School, I majored in Finance, even though I had never studied it before because it was an integral part of being a Managing Director. I knew myself well and one of my strengths was that I would study only if I had an examination to aim to pass. And this strategy got me through B School. My second strategy was to get hands-on experience in as many divisions as possible. At P&G, the structure did not allow this but I waited for my opportunity. While I waited, I did well in Finance and spent my spare time with my friends, Vivek and Dippy, who taught me about marketing and field operations. When Gurcharan Das, the Managing Director of P&G, proposed to build a leadership bench by rotating potential leaders through the divisions, I was the first to raise my hand. After five years moving between departments in Finance, I moved to the Marketing and Sales division.

The Offer from L'Oréal was tempting, but to take it on I would have to face my fear of building a start-up from a franchise. I approached ASK Rangan, my friend, Girish's, father for advice. I loved the way he framed his questions: "What are you afraid of?" *My failure.* "What if you succeed and build a robust L'Oréal in India." He advised me to accept ambiguity and said I needed to prove some things to myself to build my confidence. In accepting the L'Oréal offer, I learnt that life is full of uncertainty and that I needed courage. The world's most successful people often exemplify great courage. They are willing to take risks in the face of failure. Research suggests that courageous people use positive emotion to overcome fear. People with the potential for success are better able to accept ambiguity and cope with the unexpected. They are flexible and ready to adapt. What I learned from L'Oréal and Airtel was that working in the grey zone is also energising and fun.

Balance risk with common sense – being cautious and pragmatic pays off.

Value diversity and build a culture of inclusion and engagement.

Be flexible and adapt – you don't know what the market is going to throw at you.

Reframe difficult situations – see them as opportunities to learn and grow rather than obstacles in your path.

Be curious. Look for things that grab your attention and you would like to learn more about. Curiosity helps in gaining new knowledge and learning new skills more than you might think. At Airtel, we led with curiosity as every day threw up a new challenge. I was forced to unlearn what I knew and relearn what the new situation called for. It was clear that solutions that had worked for me and my teams in the past did not always work with these new challenges. We needed new ways of defining the issues, new perspectives, new skills, new structures, and new strategies. In the six years I was there, we restructured at least three times, changed our branding and logo twice, and moved from rented to owned offices in all six circles[6]. I was responsible for. We

---

[6] Each circle was a legal entity with its own licence to operate as a service provider.

outsourced our IT operations to IBM, our tech operations to Ericson and Nokia Siemens, and our call centres to partners across the country. Alongside all of this, we expanded our network to every village in the country and aimed for zero error tolerance levels in all migrations to new systems with our partners. We grew our top line to over two billion dollars and some of my circles had an EBITDA margin of over 60%. *Oh boy, it was pure fun!!* All this was possible only because of the adaptability and agility of our team.

My biggest lesson was to *challenge myself.* Pursuing a goal that is achievable but not easy is a great way to stay motivated to succeed. Challenges keep you interested, improve your self-esteem, and accept constructive feedback. Choosing a task that is a little challenging will motivate you to get started – it's exciting!

Co-create the differentiator

Doing things alone is difficult. In my opinion, it's impossible. Build a strong team. Having a strong support system will make things easier. Coaches, mentors, friends, co-workers, and family members can cheer you on when things get tough and offer advice and assistance that can help improve your chance of success. My wife, Anjali, has been my strongest supporter and my biggest critic.

At L'Oréal, I honed my recruitment skills by recruiting the first hundred or more employees. If nothing else, I learned that recruitment takes time and requires zero tolerance for error. I often asked myself, have I let the best candidate go? I was convinced that K Srinivas was the right person for the post of CEO of the Andhra Pradesh Circle for Airtel. But in the hour, we spent together, Srini was not convinced.

I asked him to join me for a drink that evening and spent time answering his every question in detail to convince him. In contrast, I was convinced that Shankar Prasad was the right person for the job within the first five minutes of our breakfast meeting, and so was he. There are times when you might headhunt someone you have seen working and strategising in the market. I knew we needed Elango and asked him to meet me for a drink at Bangalore Club and offered him the CEO position for our Kerala circle.

"Happy Employees make Happy Customers"

Ask any marketing guru about the time they invest in creating differentiators. At Airtel, I realised that the real differentiator in the market was our people. I learned that a diversity policy focused on representation can neglect the unique traits each of us bring. The belonging and engagement of employees' experience at work are integral to creating the differentiator. When engagement is high, performance improves and so does the bottom line. When employees trust their employer, they step forward and do their best. People align around a common purpose and take risks, think outside the box, and communicate openly and honestly. Without trust, people jockey for position, hold back information to protect themselves and play it safe. Everyone wants to bring their authentic self to work, and this underlies our need to belong. But when trust is lacking and people clamp up, they shut themselves out, they are less engaged, and performance suffers. Every leader needs to build on human capital to create the differentiator and its advantages. Humanise the organisation.

Take control when it is needed. It can be difficult to stay intrinsically motivated to pursue a goal if you don't feel that you have any real influence over the outcome. Look for ways that you can take an active role and don't fear competition. There might be other people out there trying to reach the same goals but that doesn't mean you should give up. Don't compare your progress or journey with others'. You have your own journey and your own path to carve. Nurturing a healthy sense of competition can motivate successful people, but avoid falling prey to jealousy. By focusing on your challenges, rather than on being the best leader, you will progress.

I have always spelt success with 5Cs

In my journey of close to thirty years in industry and fifteen years as a consultant and executive coach, I have always looked for a framework to help me stay on track for success. I found my framework for success with the 5Cs and later named our firm Enterprise5C.

Character is integrity combined with conviction, understanding, courage, loyalty, and respect. At an organisational level, character is reflected by governance and is evident in the culture of the organisation as much as in leadership behaviour.

Commitment is to play to win. When your positive character drives this, it naturally becomes a win/win situation that is about making sure both parties win. Commitment is based on integrity and wisdom. Wisdom guides us to know what we are capable of delivering, and integrity pushes us to deliver what we have committed to.

Consistency is about making excellence a habit. Every team member, every employee, looks to leaders for consistency. Consistency in our approach, what we say, our actions, our fairness, our relatedness, and our emotion. One simple strategy for consistency is to be vulnerable, transparent, and honest. Demand rigour and discipline from yourself and you will seek consistency.

Collaboration is building long-term relationships to generate exceptional results. Connecting with others will build synergy within a team and clarifying expectations is the key to co-creating a win/win outcome. A major lesson for me was that collaboration allows unexpected leaders to emerge and we need to appreciate that anyone can lead with their strength.

Communication is one of the most important ingredients. As leaders, we need to communicate to clarify, to understand, to motivate, to connect, to co-create, and to learn. We also need to communicate our vulnerabilities. Communicate, communicate, communicate. It has always helped me to err on the side of over-communicating.

For communicating with a larger audience, I used structures that included quarterly employee forums, monthly customer meetings, and annual appraisal of my performance by all employees. These structures helped me to bond and clarify. Conversations are meaningful next steps as we learnt at "Airtel Dialogues". Tools like SCARF and Communication Quotient will help to sharpen your communication, and keeping lines of communication simple and precise will build alignment and conviction within a team.

Believe in your future to join the dots

To create the future, you need to believe in your dream, visualise it, and find the courage to follow your path. As Thomas Edison said, "Opportunities come dressed in overalls," and one needs to work hard. Working hard by energising and living your dream will bring you immense happiness. Try to learn from your successful heroes by looking for the courage they showed in working for their goals. The future belongs to those who dare, show courage, and are ready to step outside their comfort zone. Remembering that you have set your own limits will help you to be fearless in thought and action. If you take complete ownership of the consequences, you will find the twinkle in your eye, the song in your heart and your smile will always greet others.

If you are reading this book to help release the hostage, you are already privileged. Privileged that your journey started some time ago and you are now energised and committed to achieving even greater heights. Express your gratitude and look forward to the future with enthusiasm. Remember that you have only three things in your control. Your perceptions, your decisions, and your actions. Happiness is not something you plan in the future, so live in the moment and be happy now. Be at the speed of presence.

Create your big picture, your own future. Acknowledge, appreciate, accept and allow your future to unfold. You will find that your picture will evolve and the pieces will align as you move forward with courage and confidence. May you be blessed with enough.

AUTHORS BIO

Jagdish is a high impact, highly disciplined, and a very passionate leader. Has always led from the front and takes pride in shaping his career with many success stories. Till the age of 20 his biggest goal and other subsidiary goals failed. He soon discovered that dreaming big is just not enough.

His business career started in 1976 when he joined Siemens India as a trainee in the plant at Kalwe, Thane near Mumbai. During the three and half years he worked at Siemens he had the opportunity to observe professionals from close quarters and he chartered his career starting by equipping himself with an MBA. His campus recruitment gave him the opportunity to work at Procter and Gamble.

He grabbed the offer to set up L'Oréal in India when it was offered to him. His leadership skills helped to establish the company in India with a strong base. During the seven years that he led the company he was able to build a strong team with an attitude to win. The team at L'Oréal in a way revolutionized the packaging for FMCG products, and scored with many successful launches, in skin care, hair care and hair care fashion. It was the first FMCG company to establish a 100% subsidiary in India. It was in this phase that he was able to sharpen his entrepreneurial skills.

He was sponsored to INSEAD to equip himself with an Advanced Management Program this prepared him for the responsibility of being the Managing Director, at Gillette. After a couple of M&As and leading the India operations for close to 4 years the mid forty blues were hitting him hard. He questioned his own role in business, and his impact on society.

It was at this stage in his life he met with Sunil Mittal who explained his vision that he had for Airtel, a company which was recently launched in the mobile telecom space. On the other side of the same coin Jagdish saw his purpose. His purpose to change the way the average Indian Lived. Telecom revolution was in its infancy. His dream was big, but it was worth the chance. The rest as they say is history. As Executive Director and CEO of the company he was able to establish Airtel as a frontline company and an undisputed leader in the market, that set new benchmarks for the industry not only in India but for the Global telecom markets. It was during this six-year period he coached his team members to become visionary leaders for the future. The bench of future leaders that he created is still a matter of pride for him. In his career spanning close to 30 years in different organisations he has visited over 50 countries and has had postings and project work in some of them.

Two months before he turned 50 years old, he decided to move his cheese. A goal he had taken on for himself when he graduated from B school. Besides acting in a play, he did different things to keep him going. He did try new things as one of his values is to be a learner for life. With his wife as the partner, he started the consulting firm Enterprise 5C. In the last 15 odd years E5C has had many clients some large and some not so large. Prominent among them are Tatatele (DoCoMo), Tata Power, Tata Consumer, Airtel, 3M, Vodafone,

AUTHORS BIO

Mahindra & Mahindra Group, M&M Finance, M&M Auto & Farm Div., Diageo, Ferrero Roche, GSK Health, Citi Bank, PWC, Jubilant Genesis, Jubilant Biosys, Arvind Brands, Maxis, Obopay, MTN, among others.

Having done a lot of Strategic consulting in the past decade, he now focuses and prefers to operate in the space of executive coaching and leadership development. This is where he derives maximum satisfaction. He has coached over 200 CXOs and senior leaders in the industry in the past 9 years. He is a certified coach, PCC (ICF certified) and is the Past President of the ICF Bangalore Chapter. He is a global resource coach with CoachA of Japan, Acuity – London and TLC -USA.

He has studied his coaching rigor from RCS a school run by Franklyn Covey and David Rock. He has also trained under Marshall Goldsmith, and has learnt deep intensive coaching skills from Leone Vanderpol. He is a certified facilitator for Points of You – Israel. He is certified for Lumina a psychometric tool. He has absorbed all the good from the coaching gurus but has developed his own style for coaching.

His programs "Unleash Your Potential" (3 days), "Take Charge" (1 day) and Designing Solutions (2 days) have been accepted very well across India, Malaysia, Indonesia, by his clients and others whom he has trained in the past decade. He has spent time mentoring young entrepreneurs (had his own incubation cell) and spends time mentoring youngsters from the industry through his reach out program "Coffee with Kini".

He enjoys a game of golf, with friends. His other hobbies are photography travel and dramatics. He enjoys being in the company of youngsters with whom he keeps sharing his experiences. He speaks English, Hindi, Marathi and Konkani. An alumnus of Bombay

University, SIBM (Pune) and INSEAD (Fontainebleau France) lives in Bangalore with his wife and family.

You can reach him jagdish.kini@gmail.com or on his handheld +91 98450 80000. Wish to know more about him visit jagdishkini.com

"I feel Blessed, at P&G I learned to manage and build brands. At L'Oréal and at Gillette, I learned to manage and build companies. At Airtel, I learned to build an industry".

www.ingramcontent.com/pod-product-compliance
Lightning Source LLC
Chambersburg PA
CBHW020905080526
44589CB00011B/454